S0-AXV-756

A STUDY OF THE JUNIOR CHILD

FOR JUNIOR TEACHERS

By
MARY THEODORA WHITLEY

A Textbook in the Standard Course in Teacher Training, Outlined and Approved by the International Sunday School Council of Religious Education

THIRD YEAR SPECIALIZATION SERIES

Printed for
THE TEACHER TRAINING PUBLISHING
ASSOCIATION
by
THE WESTMINSTER PRESS
PHILADELPHIA

Copyright, 1923, by
MARY THEODORA WHITLEY

Printed in the United States of America

CONTENTS

Sunday School Council Standard Course in Teacher Training

Third Year—Specialization

Third Year Specialization Courses in Teacher Training Conforming to the Standard and Outlines approved by the International Sunday School Council.

For Teachers of Beginners
A Study of the Little Child, Mary T. Whitley.
*Story-Telling for Teachers of Beginners and Primary Children, Katherine D. Cather.
Methods with Beginners, Frances W. Danielson

For Teachers of Primary Children
A Study of the Primary Child, Mary T. Whitley.
*Story-Telling for Teachers of Beginners and Primary Children, Katherine D. Cather.
Methods for Primary Teachers, Hazel Lewis.

For Teachers of Juniors
Junior Department Organization and Administration, Ida M. Koontz.
A Study of the Junior Child, Mary T. Whitley.
Junior Teaching Materials and Method, Roger Albright.
Other units in preparation.

For Teachers of Adolescents (Intermediates, Seniors, and Young People)
Psychology of Early Adolescence, E. Leigh Mudge.
Community Forces for Religious Education (Early Adolescence), G. Walter Fiske.
Organization and Administration of the Intermediate Department, Hugh H. Harris.
Community Forces for Religious Education (Middle Adolescence), G. Walter Fiske.
Other units in preparation.

For Teachers of Adults
A Study of Adult Life, Theodore G. Soares.
Principles of Christian Service, Henry F. Cope.
Other units in preparation.

For Administrative Officers
The Educational Task of the Local Church, W. C. Bower.
Other units in preparation.

---

* Identical.

4

EDITOR'S INTRODUCTION

SPECIALIZATION COURSES IN TEACHER TRAINING

In religious education, as in other fields of constructive endeavor, specialized training is to-day a badge of fitness for service. Effective leadership presupposes special training. For teachers and administrative officers in the church school a thorough preparation and proper personal equipment have become indispensable by reason of the rapid development of the Sunday-school curriculum which has resulted in the widespread introduction and use of graded courses, in the rapid extension of departmental organization, and in greatly improved methods of teaching.

Present-day standards and courses in teacher training give evidence of a determination on the part of the religious-educational forces of North America to provide an adequate training literature, that is, properly graded and sufficiently thorough courses and text-books to meet the growing need for specialized training in this field. Popular as well as professional interest in the matter is reflected in the constantly increasing number of training institutes, community and summer training schools, and college chairs and departments of religious education. Hundreds of thousands of young people and adults, distributed among all the Protestant

Evangelical churches and throughout every state and province, are engaged in serious study, in many cases including supervised practice teaching, with a view to preparing for service as leaders and teachers of religion or of increasing their efficiency in the work in which they are already engaged.

Most of these students and student teachers are pursuing some portion of the Standard Course of Teacher Training prepared in outline by the International Sunday School Council for all the Protestant churches in the United States and Canada. This course calls for a minimum of one hundred and twenty lesson periods including in fair educational proportion the following subjects:

(a) A survey of Bible material, with special reference to the teaching values of the Bible as meeting the needs of the pupil in successive periods of his development.

(b) A study of the pupil in the varied stages of his growing life.

(c) The work and methods of the teacher.

(d) The Sunday school and its organization and management.

The course is intended to cover three years with a minimum of forty lesson periods for each year.

Following two years of more general study, provision for specialization is made in the third year, with separate studies for administrative officers, and for teachers of each of the following age groups: Beginners (under 6); Primary (6-8); Junior (9-11); Intermediate (12-14); Senior (15-17); Young People (18-

24); and Adult (over 24). A general course on Adolescence covering more briefly the whole period (13-24) is also provided. Thus the Third Year Specialization, of which this textbook is one unit, provides for nine separate courses of forty lesson periods each.

Which of these nine courses is to be pursued by any student or group of students will be determined by the particular place each expects to fill as teacher, supervisor, or administrative officer in the church school. Teachers of Juniors will study the four units devoted to the Junior Department. Teachers of young people's classes will choose between the general course on Adolescence and the course on Later Adolescence. Superintendents and general officers in the school will study the four administrative units. Many will pursue several courses in successive years, thus adding to their specialized equipment each year. On page four will be found a list of the Specialization Courses available at the time of publication of this volume.

A program of intensive training as complete as that outlined by the Sunday School Council necessarily involves the preparation and publication of an equally complete series of textbooks covering no less than thirty-six separate units. Comparatively few of the denominations represented in the Sunday School Council are able independently to undertake so large a program of textbook production. It was natural, therefore, that the denominations which together had determined the general outlines of the Standard Course should likewise coöperate in the production of the required textbooks. Such coöperation, moreover, was necessary in order to command the best available talent for this important task, and in order to insure the success of the total enterprise. Thus it came about that the denominations represented in the Sunday School Council, with a few exceptions, united in the syndicate production of the entire series of Specialization units for the Third Year.

A little more than two years have been required for the selection of writers, for the careful advance coördination of their several tasks, and for the actual production of the first textbooks. A substantial number of these are now available. They will be followed in rapid succession by others until the entire series for each of the nine courses is completed.

The preparation of these textbooks has proceeded under the supervision of an Editorial Committee representing all the coöperating denominations. The publishing arrangements have been made by a similar committee of denominational publishers likewise representing all the coöperating churches. Together the editors, educational secretaries, and publishers have organized themselves into a voluntary association for the carrying out of this particular task, under the name *Teacher Training Publishing Association*. The actual publication of the separate textbook units is done by the various denominational Publishing Houses in accordance with assignments made by the Publishers' Committee of the Association. The enterprise as a whole represents one of the largest and most significant ventures which has thus far been undertaken in the field of interdenominational coöperation in religious education. The textbooks included in this series, while intended primarily for teacher-training classes in local churches and Sunday schools, are admirably suited for use in interdenominational and community classes and training schools.

This volume, *A Study of the Junior Child,* intended for Junior teachers, is one of four units designed for teachers of children nine to twelve years of age. Dr. Whitley's name is a sufficient guarantee of the accuracy of its psychology. But the great value of this work lies in the fact that, while it gives a most scholarly presentation of the Junior child as he is, it does so with a charming simplicity of style and in language unencumbered by technicalities. As a textbook this work cannot fail to interest as well as render valuable service to all who are dealing with the boys and girls in this important and strategic period of life.

For The Teacher Training Publishing Association,

HENRY H. MEYER,

Chairman Editorial Committee.

For The Westminster Press,

JOHN T. FARIS,

Editor.

CHAPTER I

THE JUNIOR AS REVEALED IN THE PLAY GROUP

You are teaching, or preparing to teach, in the Junior Department of the Sunday school. Some superintendents regularly plan to start new teachers there with the classes just promoted from the Primary Department, thinking that children of that age are probably the easiest for beginners on the staff to handle. Sometimes young teachers feel hesitant about tackling classes of older boys and girls, thinking that they need further preparation themselves in the subject matter of what they are to teach, but feeling quite willing to try the fourth or fifth grade, since they are more familiar with the less extensive curriculum usually found there. Here they are guilty of failing to recognize that there is another problem in the art of teaching than simply knowing the things to be taught, namely, knowing the children who are to be taught, and the best methods of helping them develop into Christian citizens.

This book is meant to point out to you certain characteristics of boys and girls from nine to twelve years of age, so that you may be better able to bring to them the inspiration and the training that they need in this period of their growth. We are going to study children of Junior age by noting how they act and observing what they like to do. We must follow them as they show themselves in action at home, at school, and at play. Then we will consider certain traits which are specially significant in view of our interest in religious education.

If you think back to when you were a child and recall your companions at that time, do you feel you came to know them better by what you saw of them in the schoolroom or by what you found out as you played with them? And how is it with children you wish to know now; would you understand them as individuals better if you watched them at school or at play? Since most people feel that the greatest revelation of character comes during the spontaneous play activities we will observe them first in these.

Observation.—Plan to spend several different half hours watching children of Junior age at free play; in the play ground, in somebody's back yard, on vacant lots, on the streets, indoors as well, if you can, but anywhere will do. Look for any differences in the kinds of play chosen most often by boys and girls; or do they play exactly the same sort of things? Do they play together most of the time or only occasionally? You will probably see more groups of boys together and girls together than mixed groups of boys and girls; for at about ten or eleven years of age, if not before, there seems to be a decided sex antagonism, so that they prefer the company of their own kind. On the whole boys are playing more active and rougher games continually than the girls are, in spite of the tomboy tendencies many girls exhibit. But don't take

·these statements for granted. Count the groups you see in each half hour as you walk slowly through the streets, and write down of how many children the groups are constituted, whether they are mixed or of one sex only, and try also to describe just what the occupation is. Of course the time of year will make some difference. You remember that just as football has its season, so also have tops, skipping ropes, bonfires, to say nothing of the special activities suggested by the climate itself, such as snowballing, or wading in the gutter.

Next, note whether the play involves much muscular activity or not. Would you describe it as violently active, moderately so, or quiet? Chasing games we would call active, constructive work such as carpentering would be moderate, sitting down games would be classed as quiet. If your observations are made out of doors in the winter season you may not see any quiet games; but do not let the limiting conditions of your particular opportunity lead you to generalize rashly about play interests in the Junior age. Supplement your work by comparing notes with others, by recalling your own childhood, and by consulting some authorities such as those suggested in the bibliography given at the end of this book.

After noting the physical characteristics of the play activities try to analyze them from the point of view of the chief attraction on the intellectual side. For instance, how many times did you see (1) a very definite effort to gain skill? That is a prominent feature of hopscotch, jackstones, and the like. (2) Is there a repetition of the activity for the pure joy of the sensations involved, as in swinging, coasting? When you see children doing the same thing over and over watch carefully to see if you can tell for which of these two reasons there is so much repetition; is it to practice a "stunt," or is it to feel the joy of the motion? (3) List all the times that the interest seems to be principally in the æsthetic pleasure afforded—for example, you may see careful arrangements of colored leaves, embroidery work, in fact all sorts of creative work involving decoration. Distinguish this from (4) the construction in which little heed is paid to the looks of the thing when finished, but in which the interest is in the mechanics required, in the act of making something, or in the further use to which the object made can be put. Where, among these four groups would you class jumping rope, playing a mouth organ, whittling, building a playhouse out of waste lumber, doll's dressmaking? (5) Notice any plays that bring in the dramatic imagination. What is the source of the things children act out is it everyday life around them, or books they may have read, the more unusual scenes of the circus or what? Are they the traditional games such as fox and geese, with very little original imagination left in? (6) How often did you see rivalry and competition as a marked feature of the game? (7) Was there any play that showed the love of puzzles? Guessing games, language games with pencil and paper, board games such as checkers, many card games are good examples of this "solve a problem" interest. We might analyze still more of these intellectual features, but these seven are the most significant. Let us review them: interest in gaining skill, sensory enjoyment, æsthetic pleasure, constructive interest, dramatic imagination, competition, problem-solving. We will symbolize these by Sk., S., A., Con., D., Cp., P., respectively. Many plays will give pleasure through two or three of these factors at the same time; thus, we might characterize building a snow fort by the symbols Con., D., and Cp.

Having observed the physical and the mental sides of play let us turn now to the analysis of the social organization. Here we may distinguish five types. First, individualistic play, where a child plays by himself. Second, the undefined group, where any convenient number may join and all do nearly the same thing at the same time; for example, in "going to Jerusalem," "cross tag," and much doll play. Third, the double group where two undefined groups compete as in "tug of war," "prisoners' base." Fourth, the pair or double pair, exemplified in tennis or checkers. Fifth and last, the organized team game, where two sides compete as in type three, but now the numbers on each side are limited by rule, and each member of the team has a specialized task, even a special name by which he is known. Of course hockey and baseball are good examples of this, and you can easily think of others. Be sure you get these five social organizations clearly in mind. To which does "drop the handkerchief" belong? Hide-and-seek? Basket ball? Playing circus? Top-spinning? Jackstones? Be careful when you see eight or ten boys with bats and balls, that you watch their play long enough to decide whether it is really a game of type five they are playing, or a simpler sort of ball game with little or no team work, any number on a side and a few rules, relegating their social organization really to type three.

To sum up. You are asked to observe children of nine to twelve playing, during several different half hours, and to note carefully the following: A. The size and sex of the group. B. The approximate age within the limits given. C. The physical features. D. The intellectual features. E. The social organization. The results of your observation can be conveniently arranged in tabular form in six columns. Let b 5 in column A mean that the group consisted of five boys, whereas, g 4 b 1 would mean a group of four girls and one boy. Let A. M. and Q stand for active, moderate and quiet respectively in column C. Use the symbols suggested above for the various intellectual features in column D. Let 1, 2, 3, 4, 5 stand for the type to which you assign the social organization, in column E.

A sample record may look like this then:

Activity Described	A Size, Sex	B Age	C Physical	D Intellectual	E Social
Dam in a gutter; wading; sailing boats....	g 3 b 4	9–12	M	S. Con. D. Cp.	2
Baseball..............	b 7	10–11	A	Sk. Cp.	3
Doll dressmaking......	g 5	9–10	Q	Sk. A.	2
Roller skating........	g 1	10	M	Sk. S.	1

Can you follow all these letters and figures, and interpret? Observe long enough to get a list of thirty or more activities if possible, and tabulate your findings in the way demonstrated here. Compare your results with those of the other members of the class, and then see if you can decide on an answer to these queries. (1) Is rivalry or competition a marked feature or not? Kirkpatrick has called this age part of the competitive socialization period; if that is a good term we should expect to find a great deal of competition in the free play life. (2) Do the games have many rules? (3) How often is there a definite problem interest beyond that of gaining physical skill? (4) Do children under twelve play team games, of type five, spontaneously? Do girls? Is there cheerful obedience to a captain with coöperation towards a definitely planned goal?

General characteristics peculiar to this age period. —Now that you have worked over these suggestions for a while we will gather up what other investigators have noticed as to the play interests of this period.

From ten to eleven years old is apparently the time when the greatest variety of games and amusements is enjoyed. This is probably because children still like many sorts of games they played when smaller, and also are beginning to appreciate the kind that older boys and girls play. It is also a time when many traditional games are in favor; in fact, very few new games are invented, whereas the imitative tendency is sufficiently strong for them to pick up from one another all the many plays current, and thus to come into their inheritance of folk ways of which there is so vast an accumulation through the ages. There is a decreasing interest in make-believe plays and an increasing interest in games of chance, or chance and skill both. Games involving mere chasing decline in favor, but games with balls rise rapidly in value. Rivalry, competition or contest enter into almost everything they do in groups. This element of personal rivalry is so much stronger, in fact, than the team spirit, that many a so-called group game proceeds but lamely on its way because of the frequent altercations that develop. Individual interests predominate over the idea of coöperation which calls for self-sacrifice for the good of the group. Each player wants to star, even if loyalty to his own gang or side makes him desirous of seeing it beat the other side.

Physical activity.—About two thirds of all their games involve considerable bodily movement. Running and ball games are not the only ways of indulging in violent physical exercise; it is decidedly the age of stunts, when children will practice faithfully at some activity to attain speed or accuracy. Shouting is so frequent an accompaniment of play that many adults think of play and noise as almost synonymous terms. At the same time, quiet employments, such as board games, table games, card games are more and more appreciated as they are better understood, while quiet puzzle games involving language-guessing are much enjoyed in the latter part of this age period. We must not omit mention of the very prevalent habit of attendance at the moving-picture theater, with its relatively slight use of the larger muscles.

Language interest.—Conundrums, puns, word-building, "how-when-and-where," "telegrams," and many other similar plays help develop the quickly growing appreciation of language. Generally, too, we find that some sort of secret language is invented by eleven or twelve years. In oral form this may be of the dog Latin variety, *i. e.,* some modification of the mother tongue made by adding syllables to ordinary words, changing the sequence of syllables or letters, pronouncing them backwards or whatever variation their ingenuity may suggest. Thus used, it serves to mystify the younger children and keep all but the members of the secret society from knowledge of what is being said. Akin to this is the love of passwords, mystic signals, finger-talking, and the like. More rarely there is a written form invented. This usually takes the form of a letter code into which the mother tongue vocabulary is transliterated. Again the purpose is to effect private communication.

Collecting.—Another dominant interest is that of collecting. One investigator found that at ten years old any child may be collecting four or five different sorts of things at once, also that over 90 per cent of children collect something or other. Cigar tags, small pictures, buttons, bits of metal, smooth pebbles, colored glass, shells, birds' eggs, advertisements, marbles, seaweed, stamps, paper dolls—all these and many more prove attractive objects to children at this time. Very seldom is there any serious attempt to classify the hoard. When there is any arrangement it is on some crude basis of size, or color, with little real insight into the nature study material that may have been amassed. However, the size of the collection itself seems a very important matter, stimulating much rivalry and not a little sharp bargaining. On the whole, the interest in marbles is dying out, that in stamps is only beginning by eleven years old. Boys are more apt than girls to collect parts of animals—claws, teeth, tails, etc., even small living things themselves, while they leave to girls the acquisition of stray pieces of silk, velvet, ribbon, cloth, paper patterns, paper dolls, perfume samples, and so on. Girls more often depend upon finding, buying, or having their treasures given them; boys, more aggressively, go on the hunt for them and barter fiercely with each other.

Sex differences.—Among other ways in which boys and girls differ we note that girls are rather more sensitive than boys to æsthetic arrangement of material, and to the beauty of rhythmic movement. They are considerably less interested in the mechanics of things, so that their constructive work runs less to experimenting with building materials, electrical apparatus, or carpenter's tools, such as boys prefer, and more to the use of textiles, pottery, paintbrushes, and so forth. They play with dolls up to eleven or twelve, not as the little girl of four or five plays, but in more complex ways, such as giving a play in which the dolls are actors, planning and making extensive wardrobes for various characters in a community life, carrying out a sort of serial story from day to day with the dolls as participants. Often there are large collections of paper dolls which replace the more realistic playthings.

On the whole, girls like running games and ball games less than boys do, and are earlier interested in games of chance. They play indoors more than their brothers, and so are apt to be more quiet and less affected in their occupations by change of season. They are less likely, when they quarrel, to engage in the violent rough-and-tumble fight which the more pugnacious boys find so necessary to determine supremacy. We should be surprised, too, to see a swarm of girls engaging in a pitched street battle with a rival swarm; but we look upon such affrays among boys with unconcern, finding them a perfectly natural occurrence. In a later chapter we shall have more to say about the gangs boys form, about chumming and friendships, only remarking here that a great deal of the activity of boys over ten is determined by the interests of that gang to which almost every one of them belongs.

Analysis of playthings.—Looking at their activities from the point of view of what sort of objects interest them and why, we can follow Woodworth's [1] classification of toys to some extent, as follows: There are: (1) Models of articles which adults use. Toy boats, dolls and their accessories are good instances of these. (2) Things that make a noise, such as firecrackers, whistles, things to be shaken, banged or struck, and the more primitive forms of musical instruments. (3) Things that increase one's speed in moving. Roller skates, sleds, bicycles, swings belong in this class. (4) Things giving one power at a distance. The water pistol, pea shooter, flash mirror, bow and arrow, sling shot, bats and balls of several sorts are illustrations of this. And here surely is one explanation of the absorp-

---

[1] Woodworth. Psychology, Ch. 19.

tion in listening in by radio to things which if spoken or sung in the same room would not be particularly interesting. (5) Things that seem to disregard the force of gravity. Here belong kites, bouncing balls, balancing tops, soap bubbles. The exhilaration of going up in the Ferris Wheel, even of swimming and floating, comes partly from this. (6) Plastic materials, or things to be manipulated and managed, illustrations being boards and tools, paper, cloth, snow, clay, meccano sets, even fire. It would be well to list the things with which you played between nine and twelve years of age, and see under which class you would place them. Some things doubtless would be classified in more than one way; the favorite playthings made an appeal for more than one reason.

Other instinctive interests.—The instinct of *hunting* shows in many games of pursuit, chase, and capture, as well as in the more imaginative games of digging for treasure, Indians, and so forth. It enters also into the joy of aiming at a mark, as it does so obviously into fishing and trapping. It partly explains the delight of crude cooking at picnics, or in the gang's hang-out. The instinct of *mastery and self-assertion* is hardly ever absent from play occupations. In the cruder forms of fighting it expresses itself in the rough-and-tumble scramble, in wrestling, in the snow-fort battle of the two crowds. It is an element in all forms of sport, where the contest is primarily with nature. Overcoming the difficulties of the climb, the slipperiness of the ice, the force of the stream owes its joy to the fight involved. Scarcely a game but is competitive. Most motor skills are acquired largely with the hope of beating someone else eventually, unless the mastery of the implement itself is a sufficient struggle. Even the pleasure of gaining mental skill is deeper for the combat with difficulty it implies. The instinct of *fear* is often closely linked with this. Children—like all of us—like fearsomeness in objects, provided ultimate control is gained. Fear provides a thrill which incites either to escape and be chased, or to attack and overcome. Horrors to look at are exciting and pleasant if one can be assured of getting away from them. Dangerous exploits are attractive for the same reason, always supposing one's skill is just sufficient to overcome the danger. Fear of falling is successfully woven into the switchback railway, shoot the chutes and similar contrivances in our amusement parks. Balancing, climbing, swinging down from high boughs all contribute to the mastery impulse, as the danger is conquered by one's magnificent prowess. What wonder, then, that children simply have to brag, and to show off, and to incite each other to stunts? What wonder that the athletes of the circus are such heroes, and such stimulating examples?

The instinct of *manipulation* is strongly represented, too, in many of the activities. Sometimes we call it constructive tendency, but from the adult point of view it is just as often the destructive. So long as the hands are busy, and changes are produced in the materials upon which they are at work, it makes little difference to the boy or girl what we call it. To make things happen, to get results, is the interest, rather than the social or economic value of the result. This, allied to *curiosity*, leads to much investigation into how things are made, why things happen, what will happen if— We might well stop and ask ourselves when is mischief mischief, and when is it misdirected scientific experiment, or unskilled workmanship? When the manipulation takes the form of constructing a playhouse of sorts we recognize the influence of the instinct of *home-making*, like that of nesting in the birds. For this, the children are dependent on the structural material the environment offers. Temporary retreats in the wood pile, the haymow, the snow pile, the sand heap will do, but there is a lurking desire for more permanent shelter. If they live near woods we shall see a sort of wigwam, probably. If there is a sloping bank, a cave or a tunnel may be fashioned. The city boys utilize the vacant lots and the cast-off treasures that find their way thither in the shape of ends of board, linoleum, tin cans —which can be hammered out flat—and so forth. At this age, there is an ambition for a real door and window, perhaps a seat inside, and a contrivance for cooking. Girls are less likely to go to the trouble of building all this; they more often adopt suggestive looking alcoves, glades in the woods, corners or area ways, cubby-holes under the bushes, and imagine the rest. But they must beautify their abode in some way. Mosses, leaves and stones decorate the sylvan retreat, textiles, the urban residence. Dolls and their furniture come to inhabit the home, and the social life carried on is somewhat different in tone from that among the boys. The instinct of *social activity* is strong, too.

Children at this age far more often play together than play singly. There is satisfaction in being together, in sharing experiences of sight and sound and movement, in acting together, even if competition does not arise. The companions are always very near each other in age, as they naturally find greater community of interests and abilities in those of their own stage of development than in those much younger. The adolescents, in turn, do not want these preadolescents around with them, so that they perforce coalesce into groups of their own kind.

FOR DISCUSSION

1. In planning a party for the Junior Department, what are the chief things to be considered? Why?

2. Recall any party for Junior age children you have attended that has not been a success. Try to analyze the reason.

3. How could you enlist the fondness for collecting in the service of the Sunday school?

4. What play interests that you have seen can be used to develop interest in missions?

5. What might you learn about a child's character from watching him at play that you could not learn so well from dealing with him in a Sunday-school class? Why?

6. What valuable moral lessons do children learn from their play at this age?

CHAPTER II

THE JUNIOR AS REVEALED AT HOME

Apart from individual differences due to heredity, the conduct of children is influenced by the kind of home training to which they have been subjected. Some will show development due to having shared responsibilities, some will be as immature and helpless as children of seven in other homes. Some would do their parents credit in any company, some have manners that would disgrace a Hottentot; so much depends on the family's standards and the mother's way of managing. Racial and national customs vary considerably also, so that you would not expect to find Julia O'Brien, Liza Ann Johnson, Otto Schwegler, Louis Santi, Ten Eyck Schuyler Franklin T. Brooks, and Virginia Lee all with the same table manners, even though they have come to wear much the same sort of clothes. Neither does the child in the farm home compare directly with the child in the three-room city tenement or in the nine-room small town house, though all may be in the fifth grade in school. The city and town boys suffer more often for lack of regular assignment of duties in the home than does the country boy, whose contribution to the family life will almost surely include keeping the fuel box filled. Very seldom is a boy required to keep his room in order, to wash and wipe dishes, sweep the porch, or do the dozen other things that are generally expected from a girl. You should know your neighborhood's customs, to supplement any general ideas you may gain by the closer study of each of your pupils in the light of the home influences.

Of course, as a faithful and interested Sunday-school teacher you take occasion to visit your pupils in their homes; and you have doubtless found that you have been very much better able to understand some of them when you are familiar with the atmosphere in which they have spent their early, impressionable years, when you see the sort of standards the family maintains, and when you get acquainted with the persons in the household who have been so constantly influencing the thoughts and the emotions of the children.

"Have been" is a suggestive tense; for from eight or nine years old on children show an increasing independence, and, boys especially, a rapidly increasing tendency to be guided by the opinions of the group of their own age. With this is joined only too often a reticence about their own affairs which is regarded as secrecy, so that many a parent confesses that his boy ten to eleven years of age is really an enigma to him. The feeling of misinterpretation may be mutual, however, and four contributing causes of this mutual misinterpretation are here suggested.

(1) One is that the world of ten- to twelve-year-olds is somewhat isolated after all. They have outgrown many interests that held them up to nine years old, but are not yet ready to sympathize with the adolescents' point of view. The teen-age people scorn their company, as they in turn scorn that of the seven-

year-olds. Unless the younger children arouse a kindly, protective type of behavior they are felt as a check or a drag on the many activities in which these Juniors wish to engage. As for adults, many of their actions are simply unintelligible. Adult motives leading to industrial economy, to gaining desired social reputation, and to love-making are not yet in the least appreciated. Children regard the conduct resulting from these motives, when they are conscious of it at all, as boring, or as highly ridiculous. When it comes to the actions of adults toward themselves, children are apt to feel, uncomfortably but vaguely, that these are sometimes unjust but seldom to be foretold. True, older people are convenient sources of pocket money, also of clothing, food and other necessaries which are taken for granted; but the occasions of their wrath are scarcely to be predicted, their attitude towards delightful occupations is quite uncertain; consequently, a general defensive reserve proves the best policy. Why, when two boys fall in the stream and get their clothes soaked, was a scolding the immediate result? Since it was, they do not betray the next accident, which unfortunately leads to serious consequences by not being dealt with at once. Why does one adult appear interested, even commendatory, on observing some constructive experiments, while another shows nothing but exasperation?

(2) Another big reason for misunderstandings is that their sense of ownership is but imperfectly developed. Though they resent having their own possessions taken by others or injured in any way, they do not hesitate to use freely anything that is convenient

when they are busy investigating, regardless of whose it is. At home, too, many things are used in common; and unless specific directions have been given as to whether they may or may not help themselves without permission, or make use of certain articles, they are not likely to stop and ask, when the need of carrying out some plan is urgent.

Several studies of the spontaneous growth of the sense of ownership during this age period reveal the following facts: (*a*) Possessions held in common by a large group of children are carelessly treated, no personal feeling of responsibility developing. If a group from another locality makes temporary use of these possessions, however, a real anxiety may be expressed for the careful handling, by the others, of "our" swings, our water-chute, and so forth. (*b*) A new thing found, such as a tree with a bird's nest, is looked upon as belonging to the one who first finds it, provided he marks it in some way. This individual ownership is respected by the rest for the period of immediate interest, in this case for the season. (*c*) An article bought by a child out of money he has saved or earned is felt, both by himself and others, to belong to him specifically. (*d*) An object on which labor is expended is regarded by the child as his, whether or not he paid for the materials used in the labor. He resents other people's careless treatment of such an object. Other children do not necessarily regard the object as his unless they sympathize with the effort in the labor. The brass door handles *I* cleaned, *my* steps that *I* scrubbed must not be wantonly soiled by the other children in the orphanage. (*e*) Food in bulk, in the cellar, ice box or pantry shelf does not belong to the purchaser so much as to the willing and hungry child; but food once served on the individual plate is "mine." (*f*) Goods bestowed by routine on several of the group are seldom distinguishable. Handkerchiefs, scarfs, hair ribbons, are easily transferable. Things that fit only one, such as rubbers, overcoat, et cetera, are obviously the wearer's. When individual choice has entered in there is greater joy in possession by the owner, and greater respect of property rights by others, but very definite oversight is generally necessary as to temporary individual use of such things as towels, soap, brushes. (*g*) Gifts belong especially to the recipient in proportion as he or she likes the gift.

(Compare our adult attitudes towards (*a*) civic property in the parks, (*b*) a seat in a train, (*c*) intricate plans we have organized and worked at.)

In other words, children use a thing that they want as and when they want it. Their first sense of property comes in connection with what they themselves own, whether by discovery, use, purchase, choice, creation. Their idea of the rights of others is of later and slower development. They may be forced to recognize others' rights by their resentment when they infringe; they may appreciate others' rights if motives similar to their own have obviously actuated them. Where their group consciousness is narrow, they will seldom realize the property rights of a large group, such as the library, the school, the town. These may be represented for them in some one personality who urges care of possessions. When they are in a hurry, and greatly attracted by some article they will generally use it, very little deterred by their sense of others' ownership. Here is the cause of much social trouble.

(3) Further, children's sense of fitness of time and place is not at all the same as that of grown-ups. They are so much more impulsive that when an idea strikes them they want to carry it out at once, irrespective of the appropriateness of the occasion.

(4) Again, there is keen delight in being a cause, in seeing things happen both in the inanimate world and in the world of animals and people. The excited behavior of others is nearly always interesting to watch. Since either fear or anger makes both animals and people act in excited fashion, it is easy to see how deliberate teasing may be a delightful pastime. When angry grown-ups lose their dignity and conduct themselves in all sorts of ludicrous ways, it is evident there is no very great distance to cover from merely heedless action which may irritate adults to well-planned mischief to see them get "fussed." The following instances of children's behavior will illustrate these various points:

(a) Two little girls, ten and nine, decided to give their mother a surprise. They dressed up the cat and dog, borrowing for the purpose what looked to them like dirty lace, arguing that they used soiled towels sometimes on the dog, so, as the lace was dirty, it didn't matter. They pushed the animals into the parlor where guests were being entertained, and watched their antics from the hall. Unfortunately the chasing around resulted in tearing the valuable lace costumes.

(*b*) Several children playing circus used the backs of chairs and the bottom rails of beds as gymnastic apparatus. A pyramid of chairs on the bureau top, a clothes line tight rope from gas fixture to window-catch and other acrobatic stage properties wrought disastrous results on the furniture.

(*c*) A boy of ten delighted in teasing his fourteen-year-old sister and her friend, and jeered at all their threats. One device was to lie in wait behind a billboard with a pile of stones. As they rounded the corner of the road on their bicycles, he managed to hit the front wheel enough to make the rider swerve. Another plan was to find where his sister kept the diary in which she wrote at length, borrow it and memorize parts which he would quote at table, or in any company where he thought it might prove embarrassing to her.

(*d*) Ten-year-old Clare took pity on some ducklings that had no place to swim. She caught five and placed them in a tub of water in the yard. As it was a chilly March day and the ducklings had been hatched less than a week they all succumbed.

(*e*) Perry and Charles, excited by the events of Christmas morning started a game of tag around the dinner table just set and specially decorated. A wild clutch at the corner, and—picture the rest.

(*f*) Stuart's mother, with many invitations out to a tea for which there were extensive and intricate preparations, waited all the afternoon with curtains drawn and the lights on, listening to automobiles arriving, stopping and driving away again, but without depositing any guests. Later it was found that Stuart and two friends had attached long crepe streamers to the door, and were having lots of fun watching developments.

(g) Margaret and Jack waited until their neighbors—two elderly maiden ladies—were sure to be at home and likely to be looking out of the side window. Then they enjoyed walking the fence rail by the newly sown lawn, as the ladies could usually be relied on to come out in great agitation and caution them off.

Interest in life processes.—Another reason children and parents grow apart is on account of the latter's not keeping pace with the curiosity that is ever questioning about things only partly understood. Particularly is this true with regard to sex information. Some parents believe they can keep children ignorant, and hush up all queries on the subject; some are too embarrassed to talk about such matters; some evade the truth, or try to put the children off with a mixture of myth and falsehood which they outgrow by the time they are eight. Whatever the cause, it is unfortunately only too true that a very large proportion of boys gain their sex information from quite unclean sources, perhaps from older boys who are partly misinformed, widely curious, and who delight in shocking and perverting the younger ones. Scarcely a boy of ten but knows more than his sister a year or two older does, not simply of the reproductive processes, but also of vice, obscenity and depravity. We sometimes find girls of twelve who have been given no warning whatever of the pubertal changes they may shortly expect; but happily, girls are more often safeguarded by their mothers with clean, wholesome knowledge than left to the fears and superstitions of ignorant friends or the chances of intuitive understanding of their own natures. Along with the greater precocity in knowledge on the part of boys goes very frequently an indulgence in a number of dirty habits shared by the companions of the gang, all unknown to the mother, perhaps guessed at but unmentioned by the father. From ten to twelve seems to be the height of this unpleasant phase of boy development —a phase tacitly recognized but seldom adequately dealt with. Early and frank dealing with children in an atmosphere of scientific interest in life processes, and reverent, modest care of one's own body and the persons of others, is the best preventive of unwholesome attitudes and obscene actions.

Neatness.—Children of this age are not noted for their orderliness, so that unless there has been very careful home training in the formation of tidy habits, you will find most of them strewing their own and common possessions anywhere that they have been using them, wherever it is convenient at the moment. On the whole girls are rather more tidy than boys, since they usually have a better eye for decorative effects; but this by no means implies that girls are noted for neatness. In any case, many of the occupations which they all find interesting create what we might call a "mess"; but then, all workmen make a litter at some stage of the proceedings. Happy are those children who have some space of their own wherein they are free to work out their projects without frequent interference because of the necessity of clearing the way for meals, for company, for other prosaic claims.

Cleanliness.—This is another virtue not found flourishing among nine- to eleven-year-olds. Here again more girls than boys are careful not to soil their clothing, but that need only mean that a very few are thus careful, for almost no boys are. Well indeed may the latter be compared to little savages, for most of the time they show an absolute disregard of personal appearance, not to mention a positive aversion to soap and water. Handwashing before meals is an unwelcome practice; and Edward, who economically wet the inside of one hand only because the rest would "do," is typical of many eleven-year-olds. During these years, if not before, children are entrusted with the care of their own bodies so far as bathing goes; but any mother will tell you it takes daily inspection on her part to see that boys and girls alike wash their necks and other parts they cannot see, and when it comes to details such as nails, ears, eye corners, etc., "eternal vigilance is the price of good habits," as one psychologist puts it.

Punctuality.—Here is another goal but imperfectly achieved at this age. If the family insists upon it children may be well on time for meals, and ready to start for school without a scramble. Such habits must be specifically trained, however; there is no guarantee that children who are punctual for some engagements will not be tardy for others, nor that constant reminders of bedtime will not be necessary for those who require no urging to the dinner table. Only too often there is a tendency forming to dawdle along, taking two to three times' the time required for any task. If unchecked, this tendency fixes lazy, loitering habits which are exceedingly difficult to overcome in adolescence and which will cause no end of social inconvenience now and later. Imaginative, dreamy children are more prone to this habit as a cause for tardiness than are those whose vitality leads them into activities so engrossing that they forget the time.

Responsibility.—Marian has a puppy for whose care, welfare and training she is entirely responsible. Except that it is not allowed to sleep on her bed it is her inseparable companion. Alan keeps rabbits in the back yard and has developed a good deal of enterprise in earning money to pay for their feed. Raymond, whose mother is "easy," keeps chickens, having had them bought for him in the first place, getting most of their food from the kitchen scraps, and charging his mother the highest market price for eggs. His father purchased the necessary lumber, then helped him and his friends in the enjoyable job of setting up and shingling the chicken house. Anna has no pets; she affects a strong distaste for cats and indifference to dogs, and thinks Alan's rabbits are dirty. She has a younger sister of five whom she delights to tease, becoming impatient when she cries. She is quick and tomboyish herself, and cannot resist poking fun at her slower, more delicate fifteen-year-old sister. Russell, who is ten, almost worships his fairy-like three-year-old sister, and is most coöperative with his mother in looking out for her welfare. John, at the same age, cannot bear to have six-year-old Jerry tagging along

with him.   Eleven-year-old Rita lives in a home where
two maids are kept, and has been taught that "the
kitchen is not the place for little girls." She has never
been called on to make her own bed and would be hor-
rified were she expected to help wipe the dishes or
to dust. Agnes, by contrast, does these things regularly and easily, and is also trusted to set the table for
meals. She is learning to bake cake, too, and is very
proud of the fact. Jean has three younger ones to
care for, and is a real little mother to them. She
amuses and tends the baby, plays with them all, helps
sew and mend for them, puts three-year-old Alice to
bed, looks after their manners at all times, and con-
voys Bobby safely over two street crossings to the
school they attend.

Thus to sum up, children of this age are usually
impulsive, heedless and irresponsible; but if their
training has placed upon them definite responsibilities, we may find habits of carefulness in social
adjustment, helpfulness, and skill in many directions.

An important factor in the development of children
is their right to money of their own. In some homes
the younger members get spending money whenever
they tease for it, provided the parents are in a good
humor. In other homes there is a weekly dole which
is promptly exchanged for candy. Tickets to the
movies can then be wheedled, errands charged for,
offerings for the collection demanded a few minutes
before the start to school on Sunday. In others a fixed
allowance is given with the express understanding of
what it is to cover; no bribes for good behavior, no tips

from an impulsively generous father, no soft-hearted cancellation of bad bargains or small debts helps eke out the income. In which type of training do you think the four uses of money are best taught, namely, how to earn, how to save, how to spend, how to give?

For each pupil then, find out all you can on the following points.

(1) Whereabouts in the family he or she comes. Are there older brothers and sisters? Younger ones? What sort of treatment is accorded your pupil by the older ones? What is the relationship between him and the younger ones?

(2) What standards of refinement are evident in the furnishings? At the table? Are the children so trained in courtesy that their good manners are automatic? Or are they self-consciously displaying "company manners?" Or are they lacking in good breeding?

(3) Are their fathers and mothers confidants of your pupils, or are they unaware of much that they do? Have they instructed them in matters of sex?

(4) What home duties devolve upon the children?

(5) Do they have a regular pocket money allowance?

(6) Is there a fixed hour for retiring? Do they keep to it?

(7) Is there any special place where the children can play undisturbed, and keep their own treasured belongings?

(8) What sort of conversation do they hear at meals? Is it gossip about the neighbors, the details of

the housewife's tasks, sporting news, the family's daily doings, current events in the world's work, politics, art, drama, literature?

(9) Are the children nagged at for faults? Are they punished? If so, how?

(10) Which of them have pets to care for?

(11) Is there any custom of family prayers, family hymn-singing, grace at table? Do the children read the Bible at home, either aloud to their mother or to themselves?

For Discussion

1. What have you found out in your visits at the homes of your pupils that would offer suggestions as to an interesting and worth-while topic for a parent-teachers' meeting? Some of the points given above for observation you would find of value for such meetings.

2. Do you find that children who are punctual at day school are on time for the Sunday-school session? If not, why not? How does the home influence count in the case of those who are frequently tardy?

3. In view of the facts cited about the sense of property rights, suggest several methods of training by which this can be helpfully developed.

4. What books on child-training could you recommend as helpful for the parents of your children to read?

See books especially by these authors.

E. H. Abbott.

Susan Chenery.

Patterson Du Bois.

Dorothy Canfield Fisher.

W. Byron Forbush.

Sidonie Gruenberg.

Wm. Lee Howard.
Edwin A. Kirkpatrick.
Wm. A. McKeever.
J. A. Puffer.
Kate D. Wiggin.
Ira D. Wile.
Are these represented in your town library?
Prepare a list of titles to accompany this list of authors' names, and become acquainted with the style, technicality and scope of one of these books. Criticise this book in some future class meeting.

CHAPTER III

THE JUNIOR AS REVEALED IN DAY SCHOOL

Fore-Exercise

Purpose. To discover the grasp of abstractions, as such.

Ask six different children, two of ten years old, two of eleven, two of twelve, the following question. Use exactly this wording and no other. Take down exactly what each says; do not trust to your memory. Ask each child separately so that no one hears the reply but yourself.

"What is justice? What do we mean by justice?" If one replies, "It means to have justice, (or to be just)" add, "Yes, but what does it mean to be just?"

A satisfactory answer might be, "Getting punished for doing wrong," or "Treating everybody just the same, no matter who they are." Unsatisfactory answers would be, "To do right," "To be honest."

Try similarly for the meanings of pardon; charity; salvation. Bring the six answers to class for comparison.

Grading.—If by "Junior" is meant children between nine and twelve years old, you would have to look for them in day school all the way through the grades; for some backward, stupid children of nine may be in the first grade, and some very bright children of twelve are away up in the high school. Indeed, we have some very unusual instances of boys of twelve being ready for college. However, such extreme cases would obviously not be fit material for any Junior Department. You are really more concerned with children who are normally in the fourth, fifth, sixth, and perhaps low seventh grades, which correspond most closely to the classes grouped in the Sunday school as Juniors. One of the first things that should be observed is the age-grade distribution, which the superintendent or grade teacher ought to be able to supply. This would show that in the fourth grade, for instance, though there are more children whose tenth birthday is the nearest than of any other age, there are also some eight-year-olds, one or two very bright children not yet eight, some nearly eleven, and a few dull ones of over eleven. Similarly for the fifth grade and the sixth; you would in all probability find a spread of four to five years in age in one grade. If the day school is large enough to permit reclassification at least every half year you may find a rather closer age range. If the school is up to date in its classification, whether large or small, it will have groupings within the grade of the brightest children, the more ordinary ones and the duller ones. These are expected to cover the minimum grade requirements in less time than usual, in the allotted time, and in rather longer than the allotted time, respectively. It would be very wise to find out the details of the grading of your particular pupils, so that you may understand the progress they are making. One half to two thirds of them, roughly, will be classed with the typical grade class, one sixth to one fourth are lagging behind or are in the slow moving section, and the same proportion carry the work so easily that they win rapid promotion if well taught, or develop bored, lazy attitudes if they are not kept up to their best level of performance.

A visit to the classroom where your pupils spend about twenty-five hours a week will put you in touch with the methods of teaching to which they are accustomed, and with their reactions to the general influences of the school. You may wonder, sometimes, if they really are the same children you meet on Sunday or whom you have seen at home and at play. They act so differently. Why is that? Partly because they form specialized habits, not general ones. Thus, though Louise is peevish and speaks fretfully at home, her voice has a very different tone quality here. Adelaide, whose room at home is perpetually strewn with clothing and toys, has a desk in perfect order. Lawrence, who chatters continuously at play, is stiff and silent. Martin who is readily absorbed in knife whittling, seems unable to pay attention to his book. Henry, who has been a terror to two successive Sunday-school teachers by his noisy ways and impish tricks, seems to be a model of deportment. Morton, who has been slouchy and uninterested on Sunday surprises you by the efficient manner in which he acts as chairman of a hastily summoned council. Children keep one set of habits for the traditional routine of the schoolroom, for the teacher during school hours, and another set for the same teacher on the street, for the group of seats in Sunday school, for the Quarterlies and hymn books, for the behavior expected or accepted from them by different people under different circumstances.

Their minds seem to function in somewhat separate compartments too. Having distinct hours set aside for history, geography, and literature, they apparently accept these studies as so disparate that when knowledge acquired in one connection is required in solving problems of presumably another branch of learning they are disturbed by the intrusion. Discussing current events one day, Alice was asked where Rome was and could not tell until a neighbor helpfully whispered, "That's geography," when the right answer was forthcoming. Wilbur was surprised to find that the Egypt of the Moses stories and the Egypt of his Africa lesson were one and the same country.

Again, children react specifically to people, finding out quickly and surely which teacher can be wheedled, and which is unlikely to put up with any fooling. They know too, who is severe, who is easy-going, who will laugh sarcastically at them, who will laugh with them in comradeship. They soon discover who must be obeyed instantly, who is willing to repeat directions five or six times with a sort of remonstrative, helpless crescendo, who may be flouted with impunity. No wonder that the different teachers cannot always believe the reputation with which children pass from grade to grade.

Another thing it would be well to look for is the standard set in the difficulty of the home assignments. One Sunday school superintendent who objected to a certain set of lessons designed for third year Juniors on the ground that ten-year-old children should be taught by having stories told them, was convinced of the possibilities of additional teaching and study methods when he saw the sort of work his own daughter did in the fifth grade at school. There the children were being accustomed to the use of dictionaries and encyclopædias; they collected pertinent clippings from several magazines and papers, drew maps, composed and staged a little play of their own, and were trained in other ways to do independent thinking and simple research. Why should we let the children think it impossible to do any home work in connection with the Sunday lesson when they take it as a matter of course that they have to work for Monday's?

What type of music do they learn? You may find they not only have easy songs at day school by which they acquire the art of reading music and of part singing, but that they are introduced to good pieces of music by classic composers. Only too often conditions are such that children accept Sunday school as the place where trashy jingles are used with any cheap harmonization so long as there is catchy rhythm, with one constant adjuration to sing louder—"Now, everybody sing!" Good music is associated in many children's minds, not with the church school and its worship, but with other environments; and this when some of the loveliest art the world knows is at the disposal of the church, and is also well within the reach of even ten-year-old children, as evidenced by the beautiful singing of some trained choirs.

In general these years in school are especially the time for training in the formal subjects of spelling, penmanship, and arithmetic, for beginning to study geography, history, and grammar from textbooks, since the art of reading· has been acquired. Children need and rather enjoy a great amount of drilling in the technique of these studies, and into this drill a good deal of rivalry enters. Boys vie with girls, two rooms of one grade jealously watch each other's achievements, members of one class compete feverishly for the honor of being "top." Marks become so important that they are striven for as ends in themselves; and often, alas, unfair means are taken to gain them. It is so easy to stimulate cheating by undue emphasis on relative standing that the use of more general grade standards by which each child can measure his own skill and thereafter strive to improve his own record is a great help in redirecting this strong instinct of competition. Some day we may have some such general objective standards for the Sunday school, in memory work, information, and habits of conduct, as we now have for the elementary and grammar grades of our public schools.

Of all the known grade norms, those that may be interesting for the Sunday-school teacher in evaluating her pupils' abilities are as follows.

Reading.—In the fourth grade, about the middle of the school year, children can ordinarily read silently and carry out the directions accurately, in from six to eight paragraphs such as this given below in five minutes of time.

Below a simple, one-inch drawing of an opened book is the following:

"This book is lying on the desk, but it is hard to

make it stay open. With your pencil draw a single straight line to represent a ruler lying across the book to hold the pages open. Be sure to make the line from one side to the other, across the book, instead of making it go up and down." [1]

Children of ordinary ability in the fifth grade could handle from seven to nine similar paragraphs in five minutes. In the sixth grade from eight to ten is the usual number for ordinary children, for the more gifted ones perhaps as many as fifteen. Of course the words in this paragraph are not particularly difficult, but the point is to measure the rapidity of the reading and the instant and accurate grasp of the sense so that no errors appear in the drawings, for instance, two lines to represent a ruler instead of what is called for. (Did you test yourself to see either how many seconds it took you to read the paragraph, or whether you were sure enough of it at the first reading to do instantly what was asked without a second look?)

This function of mental grasp from silent reading is about as indicative of general intelligence as anything else that we could test with equal ease and speed. You will do well to find where your pupils stand in a test of this sort so that you will have some idea, not only of their brightness in general, but also of how long you should allow for reading from the Quarterly or the Bible to receive an answer to a question you have put.

Speed of writing.—There is a scale of penmanship known as the Thorndike scale, showing all grades of qualities and styles from a bad, almost illegible

---

[1] Quoted from the Burgess Silent Reading Scale (form 1).

sample up to practically copperplate perfection. These samples are numbered from 4 up to 18. We can measure children by comparing their penmanship with the numbered samples on the scale, and assigning their product a number corresponding to the sample theirs resembles most closely in regularity, spacing, beauty, legibility and general style. Then by timing them, we can state that so and so writes quality 9 at the rate of 60 letters per minute. Thus we know that for grades four, five, and six respectively, at about midyear, children should write quality 8 at 50 letters per minute, quality 9 at 60 letters per minute and almost at quality 10 at 68 letters per minute. To make this quite clear you should really take opportunity to consult this scale and get acquainted with the numbered qualities. Then you again will have some guide in knowing what to expect in the way of speed and general goodness of handwriting from your group. Thus to write out such a text as "Happy is the man that findeth wisdom," or, "Thou shalt love thy neighbor as thyself," the first-year Juniors would need a full minute on the average, allowing time for dictating or for looking back to the original they are copying. The fourth-year class would take about three-quarters as long. The younger children's script would be larger, probably; and in several of our series of lesson books there is not sufficient space left after the printed questions in the Quarterlies for all they need to write. These children also require plenty of space to dispose of their arms and legs as they write. A table is far more convenient for them than the use of writing pads to hold in their laps, or even the wide arms of student chairs. The fourth-year class can get along with these last very well.

Abstract and generalized thinking.—What shall be said of the abstract ideas expressed in books children read? Do they grasp these and respond to them as well as to the direct, specific descriptions given above? Most emphatically, they do not. At best they interpret to themselves by means of a narrow, concrete illustration; at worst they pass these ideas by with foggy vision, or misinterpret. It is seldom that they can give good meanings for purely abstract terms before twelve years old. To explain "pity," one eleven-year old said, "She lost her purse; it was a pity." Another said, "The cat scratched her; it was a pity." "It's when you break something." "To cheer people up," are other samples of inadequate explanations. Notice how the particular occasion of misfortune when the phrase might have been used is associated in the children's minds with the meaning as a general thing. At twelve years old three fourths of the children can give more satisfactory definitions of terms such as "revenge," "charity," "justice," whereas earlier the thought of the action involved or the most frequent use of the word will influence their replies.

Since the mental grasp is less now than four or five years later, we find that they do not take in so much mental material in one act of attention, nor do they appreciate the inner relationships of things well enough to be able to attend to a difficult topic of thought long without tiring. These facts about attention and apperception affect their processes of reasoning in three ways. (1) Since they do not perceive likenesses and differences, except superficial ones, clearly, they tend to make poor comparisons, and thus analyze poorly. (2) Since they do not sustain attention very long, they often fail to follow out a train of reasoning to its conclusion; they would rather jump at it, generalize hastily and leave it without verification. (3) Since the range of attention is not large they are likely to see only part of an implication at once and fail to connect the parts into larger wholes for reflection. Boys reason better than girls at these ages, we note, especially in things to do with mathematics and in practical situations. Girls are superior to boys in appreciation of poetical meaning, and often in choosing the best definition out of several offered.

Other facts about imagination and memory will be reserved for description in later chapters.

Let us now watch them in school, and see what they are doing. In this sixth grade room of thirty children a history lesson is going on. On the board are four questions indicating the main points of an outline, and under each a few phrases containing suggestions of answers. The teacher asks Louise to tell what she has found about the first topic, and, nothing loath, Louise springs up and begins an animated account of a description she has read. Charles wildly interrupts, and three or four others are excitedly waving their hands, so eager are they to contribute. Robert, indeed, almost crawls up on his desk in his anxiety to catch the teacher's eye. Julia is snapping her fingers, jerking and even groaning unconsciously as she tries to force herself on the teacher's attention. During the half hour that follows eight or nine of the children seem thus in a perpetual ferment, and take really more than their share of the discussion. By contrast, five or six more raise their hands only once during the whole period, and not more than two of them are called upon. Rita is obviously not in the least interested, and is gazing dreamily out of a window. Randolph is surreptitiously making comic sketches and passing them to his chum in the seat in front. He keeps a very fair semblance of attention, however, and the teacher might never have noticed his delightful occupation had not Charles in the next seat been watching so interestedly that he was twisted halfway round, and did not hear his name called. Winifred is just as interested really, but she prefers to act Lady Disdainful. Though she is secretly envious of Randolph's gift of striking caricature she would not acknowledge that what he draws is worth more than a passing glance. By the very toss of her head she gives herself away, however. Two other children appear perfectly stolid, and give very halting replies when questioned. Apparently they have neither learned anything in preparation for the lesson nor gained anything valuable from the recitation. When the assignment for home work is developed out of a problematic point that has come up for discussion they seem rather dazed, and respond very sluggishly. Guided by the teacher, the class dictates a fair summary of the answers found to the outlined questions, and Margaret very efficiently acts as secretary, by writing this summary in the appropriate place on the blackboard.

In this next room a study period is in progress. Some are busy with arithmetical examples, others have grammar or geography books open. Look at Esther, laboriously counting on her fingers and screwing up her face as she manipulates the number combinations. Anna, self-conscious now that you are looking at her, is making a great show of turning from place to place in her grammar and importantly writing something in a notebook. John is squirming around, scowling and muttering aloud as he repeats over and over a list of geographical names he is trying to memorize. Harold has a far-away gaze. Seemingly absorbed in the map on the wall before him, could you see into the workings of his mind you would find him busy living through the stirring adventures of a voyage of discovery, perhaps, or, more likely, enacting the part of a bold, bad bandit arranging the capture and ransom of belated and lonesome travelers. Harold never gets high grades for his school work, and invariably postpones the necessary preparation as long as possible. The teacher frequently complains of his lack of application, but he has learned to protect himself from constant reprimand and accusation of inattention by assuming an air of studious quiet. Then, his body in the attitude of a good and diligent pupil, his active imagination may take to itself wings and soar far from the atmosphere of ink and erasers. He is not stupid, nor lazy; but he loathes arithmetic, particularly fractions, he sees no sense in formal grammar, and he frankly detests the constraint of the schoolroom. For him the blackboard dissolves into a transparent screen through which he follows knights in armor in their deeds of derring do. The end of the study period finds him with no school work accomplished, but in a fair state of content, since no one has molested him with absurd conundrums anent parsing.

Now they all pass to assembly. Again notice how Morton quietly marshals his line in good order, checking Randolph's mischievous tendencies and Robert's nervous jostling. Louise reveals a remarkably good piano technique as she plays a march. Rita could play well, too, if she would undertake to practice more regularly; but she reads music so quickly and easily that she rests satisfied with finding out "how it goes," rather than feels any desire for working for a finished result. No compulsion is put upon her at home to do things for which she is not inclined. Anna and Winifred manœuver so that they sit together, and ostentatiously draw away from John's clumsy feet as he all but trips over Charles. Adelaide seems alert to all that goes on, but Lawrence still wears a wooden expression, not lightening when even Martin is interested—for the first time today—as an eighth grade boy describes a radio outfit he has been setting up in his home. Esther relapses into stolidity as she fails to follow the description, but enjoys herself later on in the singing, in which she joins lustily. Charles endeavors to sing "bass," *i. e.*, an octave lower than the right pitch for the melody, and thereby induces an attack of badly suppressed giggles in Winifred and Anna. Rita and Harold are still somewhat absent in spirit, though tolerantly present in body; their outward deportment is, however, less troublesome to the teacher than that of Julia, who fidgets constantly, or Randolph, who is a center of disturbance.

When school is dismissed it is Adelaide who lingers for perhaps a chance word with Miss Forrest alone, or—wonderful thought—even an invitation to walk part way home with her, and an opportunity to carry her books. Miss Forrest comes from quite another part of the country, and her different accent and intonation have proved so intriguing that Adelaide is in a fair way to become a faithful echo. Both she and Alice vie with each other in efforts for the deportment that will attract an approving smile; and there was much secret heartburning when the valentines so painstakingly prepared by each did not win apparently equal appreciation. Alan is really quite as devoted as they are, but he could never play openly for notice, nor even condescend to be gracious in manner. When he is moved to acts of chivalry he protects his dignity as an eleven-year-old male by a gruffness that is almost fearsome, and a rudeness that would repel were it not understood for the superficial cloak that it is. After Miss Forrest had called at his home and shown some interest in his rabbits, he carefully chose the most promising young one, spent two days constructing a special hutch and carrier for it, then presented it to her with a most grudging manner and a casual remark to the effect that she could take it if she liked, he didn't want it anyhow, it wasn't much good, and rather a nuisance to look after.

Summary. (1) Character growth is by spurts, just as is physical growth, as we shall see later. Character is made up of so many habits and ideals and attitudes. Habits are specific actions in response to different specific chances to act. Thus, neatness and obedience are not general traits of character, but convenient abstract terms for bundles of hundreds of specific habits. If then the home offers ten chances to act in a neat way and the school offers twenty entirely different chances, we can understand how Adelaide is untidy in the opinion of one person, but not of the other. If the school gives half a dozen ways of reacting with responsibility and the Sunday school none, the difference in Morton's behavior may be explained. Habits of reacting must be made general by providing many similar chances to act, even though in different environments. Or the motive behind the desired reaction must be made conscious, called on frequently, and so carried over easily to serve in different circumstances. If the real motives inspiring the numberless separate acts called "courteous" are felt, there will be less need of teaching each of such separate acts. Feeling the motive will lead children to discover appropriate acts for themselves. Which was the lack in Henry's case probably?

(2) Children generalize poorly. They need much guidance in seeing any but superficial relationships, and in organizing their thinking.

(3) Competition is keen. If restricted to the quick, bright pupils the slow, dull children feel hopelessly out of it.

(4) Children are busy manipulating something all

the time. If the occupation suggested by authority does not interest them, they will find their own. Some manipulate things with their hands, some manipulate their own fancies, some manipulate other people by display, or tricks. There is no such thing as a state of inattention, however, though teachers frequently complain of it.

(5) It is a time of sex antagonism in general. Any slight attraction toward one of the same age is disguised. Attraction to an older person may be open admiration of the puppy-dog type.

(6) Some constantly overstimulated, possibly neurotic children need, more than anything else, training in calm self-control.

FOR DISCUSSION

1. Mrs. Smith came to the grade superintendent when her son first came to the Sunday school with the request that he be placed in the same class with his friend Bob, who was also in the same grade at school. Is Mrs. Smith justified? Why, or why not?

2. Mrs. Kohl complains that her eleven-year-old child is in the same class as her neighbor, who is only nine, and she thinks her child should be promoted two grades. What would you say to Mrs. Kohl?

3. What results came from the fore-exercise? What per cent of the replies were concrete illustrations? (Example of concrete illustration. To the question, "What is salvation?" the reply, "Salvation Army." To the question, "What is pardon?" the reply, "It's pardon when you say, 'Granted,' when some one begs your pardon.") Were any explanations in terms other than actions? Did any fall back on an explanation they may have memorized? Did any show a tendency to dwell

less on direct cases, or narrow illustrations, and more on the underlying similarity of cases? If so, was it the older ones who thus compared relationships?

4. In the light of the findings, how would you criticize the use of the Beatitudes as memory work for the second year Junior? When do you think the meanings involved would be appreciated? What about I Corinthians XIII?

CHAPTER IV

THE CHANGING BODY AND STANDARDS OF STRENGTH

Fore-Exercises

1. As the children come into the Junior from the Primary Department, which look bigger, the girls or the boys? In the fourth year of the Department which look bigger?

2. In your visit to the homes of your pupils what have you noted about the following points that is of significance to their physical well-being?

(a) Hours of sleep.

(b) Probability of a well-chosen diet, well-cooked food.

(c) Habits of consulting the dentist.

(d) Tendency to use patent medicines, traditional remedies, neighbors' advice.

(e) General sanitary living, ventilation, bathing, etc.

3. What sort of physical examination is given to the children by the school system where you live? How thorough is it? How often is it given? Are there any clinics attached to the school system? Do you know what is done for the cardiac cases? For the deaf? For the tubercular?

Various ages.—Besides the chronological age of boys and girls which means of course the number of years and months they have lived, we need to know something about what is called the anatomical age and the physiological age. The former refers to the physical growth actually attained by any child as related to the norm for the age determined by measuring many thousand children. For instance, a child may be chronologically nine, but so well-grown that he is constantly taken for over ten. A radiograph of the hands and wrists would show that the stage of transformation from the soft, cartilage tissue into the hard bony substance was more like that of the average ten-and-a-half child of the same sex and race; if a careful measurement of some of these bones showed the same advancement we should call the child ten and a half anatomically, though he is only nine chronologically. It is interesting that girls show a greater anatomical age at a given chronological age than do boys; and this holds true even in the case of such boy and girl twins as have been thus carefully examined.

By physiological age is meant the stage of maturity reached as shown by changes in digestion, in the eruption of teeth, but chiefly in the functional changes of the sex organs. Here there is a great variability. Even with normally grown children adolescence does not begin at the same chronological age by any means; in fact two children both eleven years old, both well developed physically otherwise, may be as much as four years apart physiologically. We do find that tall girls mature earlier than those who are short for their age, though of the girls who mature early not all are tall. By early, is meant from eleven to twelve years old, since between thirteen and fourteen is the most frequent age for girls in this climate. Nearly seven per cent of girls begin their pubescent changes about eleven, and nearly eighteen per cent more before twelve and a half. In a class of fourth-year Junior girls, then, ages eleven and twelve, you might expect one out of every five to have had her first menstruation. These same individuals will probably have begun to grow much faster also; and, what is not so generally known, they will cease this rapid increase and reach their full growth earlier than girls whose pubescence comes later. Those who mature later continue their spurt of growth longer and do not reach their full adult stature until they are further on in the teens. Precocity is not at all a sign of poor health, as is popularly believed; though, naturally, careful hygienic regulations are required for girls at this time. Early and gradual pubescence seems better in many ways than delayed and brief, perhaps violent, developmental changes which make too great demands on the nervous system, the glandular system, and the emotional life.

The same general remarks apply to boys, except that just as their rapid increase in height and weight comes a year or more later than with girls, so also does their maturation, and it occupies a somewhat longer period. Though a very few begin their pubescent changes before eleven, the proportion of boys doing so is smaller. In a fourth-year class numbering eight members you would not be likely to find even one boy whose processes of maturing were clearly evident.

Recent experimental studies show us that the physiological age and mental age are directly related. Those who are physiologically accelerated have a higher mental age, involving more mature attitudes and interests, than those of average age. Not only that, but the physiologically accelerated can do school work better than the average or undeveloped children, so that if they have been properly classified we expect to find them in somewhat higher grades. What we might call the social age is also directly related to the physiological age, the less well-developed children not being able to make the same social adjustments that the more mature ones can. There is, further, a close connection between the time of religious awakenings and the physiological age. Girls are, in general, in advance of boys in the last two years of the Junior Department in all these lines, physiologically, mentally, socially, and in religious development.

Weight and height.—Boys of nine are about 51 inches tall, the girls very slightly less. During the years from nine to twelve the growth in height is by no means regular, but shows periods of acceleration and periods of retardation. For instance, between ten and eleven a boy adds relatively less to his height than in the preceding year, while a girl had her period of slower growth from nine to ten. By twelve, a boy is somewhere about 55 inches tall; but the girl has begun a spurt of rapid growth which will continue for the next two or three years, while the boy lags behind, as it were, not beginning his spurt until a year or more later. Thus, comparing both at twelve, we shall find the average girl taller by an inch than the average boy. At either nine or twelve, however, we can prophesy who are going to be tall as adults, and who smaller in stature; for, contrary to popular opinion, people who are short as children do not make up for it by growing into tall adults. Tall children remain relatively tall, and short ones relatively short, so that an expert can foretell with great accuracy by considering the height of a child of nine, how tall he will be when he is sixteen. Again, tall children start their period of specially rapid growth young enough to reach their full stature in adolescence actually earlier than the shorter children. These latter begin their spurt a little later, and evidently do not profit by it so much. Of course heredity counts here; tall parents are more likely to have tall than short children. Do not put down a child as undersized unless you know something about the parents' stature. Then, too, there is a certain variability to be allowed for. Though the average girl of twelve may measure 56 inches, there will be some in a crowd of them as short as 53 inches, and some as tall, perhaps, as 60 inches. So with the boys, who may range from 52 to 59 inches at twelve. On the whole, a twelve-year-old girl has attained nearly nine tenths of her stature as an adult. Since boys' rapid spurt starts later, and since they are eventually taller than most women, at twelve they have reached only about four fifths of their future height as men. Boys show a greater variability in height than girls at every age except twelve.

Since the body is enlarging in three dimensions, height cannot be considered entirely apart from girth and weight. Boys and girls at nine tip the scales at about 60 pounds. Before twelve a boy will have put on approximately 17 pounds, bringing him up to rather more than half his adult weight. A girl is more precocious, and at twelve is likely to weigh five or six pounds more than a boy of the same age, averaging 83 pounds, or about two thirds of her adult weight. This increase does not take place uniformly, but is apt to alternate with a greater gain in height. It seems to be a law that rapid growth in one direction is accompanied by slow growth in another; so that while children are using up energy in growing tall they are not doing much in the way of adding to their weight. So true is this that they look for a while very lean and stretched out, with unduly long legs and arms. Later, the system compensates itself by checking its rapidity of longitudinal increase, and by adding much more weight in proportion. The stretching-out process involves a lengthening of the bones, muscles, nerves, veins, and arteries, everything in the end to end measure of the limbs. There again, one sort of material may grow faster than some of the others. If the bones race ahead of the muscles which act as their levers, then the pull on the latter may become painful, giving rise to what children call "growing pains," a sort of cramp from the tension involved. Again, if the muscles increase mostly in length rather than in girth, their relative strength is decreased, and a resulting weakness makes itself evident.

As these, and the pubescent changes also involve differences in the hip and pelvic bones it is no wonder that we so frequently notice awkwardness in gait and carriage. The rapid growth of the arms may be one cause of the clumsy movements of the twelve-year-old, since new habits of muscle coördination must be formed. When we add to these considerations the fact that the disease known as chorea, or more popularly St. Vitus' dance, is not infrequent between ten and twelve, we realize that much may be forgiven the rough, ungraceful child because of irregularities in growth.

Many nervous ways of moving are common at this period—grimaces, licking the lips, fingering the face, biting the nails, twirling small objects, or part of the clothing. Generally regarded as mere restlessness, they are signs, not so much of excess energy or of boredom, as of imperfectly developed motor control. In some cases they indicate real fatigue, and if excessive, a medical examination should be given.

On the whole this is a healthy period, the best years being ten and eleven, the more sickly ones nine and twelve, when children have either not yet outgrown earlier delicacy or are entering upon the next phase of growth. Though we may look for the usual children's diseases they are less often fatal, since the resistance to disease is high, culminating at twelve for girls, a little later for boys. According to statistics for the whole of the United States, the most frequent cause of death during these ages, except for tuberculosis, is not illness at all, but different forms of accidents.

Other measurements.—Not only in standing height but in sitting height girls gain a greater per cent of their final growth at twelve years than do boys. So, too, in the strength of the arms and shoulder muscles. But since women are shorter and not so strong muscularly as men on the average, this does not mean that eleven and twelve-year-old girls are actually stronger in the arms than boys of the same age, nor should they be expected to lift as heavy weights. Boys are uniformly stronger than girls at every age in strength of grip. Boys are superior, too, in speed of movement as measured by the rate at which they can tap on a flat surface with an instrument like a stylus. This tapping rate increases with age, boys showing the greatest proportionate increase at ten years old, while girls at the same age vary more among themselves than at other ages. Both in strength and speed the great majority of children are right handed. In accuracy and steadiness of controlled movements with the hands, there is a marked improvement in the age period from nine to twelve, boys being perhaps slightly superior to girls in this. You recall that the play interests of this period revealed practice of all sorts of feats of skill which develop speed, strength and agility, training eye and hand together in many instances.

By using the instrument called a spirometer we can measure lung capacity in terms of the largest possible number of cubic centimeters of air contained and forcefully expelled. We find that the lungs are growing slowly but steadily all through these years. In this girls are inferior to boys at every age, having only about 89 per cent of the "vital capacity" of boys. When we consider that at twelve girls are actually taller and heavier than boys we realize that at that age they have a comparatively poorer breathing possibility than at ten. The ratio of lung capacity to weight is termed the "vital index"; so that after eleven girls have a lower vital index as compared with boys. Whether this is in part explained by the difference between girls and boys in physical activity out of doors we do not know; but we do find that girls who live in the country and are encouraged to exercise in the open air develop a vital capacity more nearly like that of boys, and consequently a higher vital index. In view of the fact of the prevalence of anæmia and tuberculosis among girls later in the teens it might be well to encourage any training that will increase vital capacity and develop good breathing habits.

By nine years old children have their second set of teeth in the front of both jaws. Before ten the two teeth just beyond the "eye" teeth on each side are changing. The first molars beyond these are only too frequently found decayed by ten or eleven. These teeth make their appearance when the child is about six years old and are perhaps neglected if the parents think they are the last of the first set, instead of the first of the permanent teeth, as is really the case.

During these years children require about sixty per cent of the food ration of an adult. At ten years the daily food value should approximate 1900 calories, about 30 calories per pound of body weight. Their diet should be plain, but abundant, and bulky rather than concentrated, since they seem perennially hungry. As for need of sleep, some authorities recommend ten to twelve hours; but very few children, as shown by statistical returns from various localities, get anything like that amount. From ten hours at nine years old to seven and a half hours at twelve years old is the more frequent habit; but the variation is wide, depending on such factors as city or country life, the family custom and standards, the hours of meals and so forth.

Why should we know these things? One reason is that we have a duty to children as whole, indivisible beings, not simply to that aspect of them which we term religious development. We need to know how they live at home, how they function socially, if we would help them live Christ-like lives. If by ignorance or carelessness the family does not promote the well-being of the children it becomes the duty and privilege of the teacher to suggest better ways of living, remedies if need be, certainly conservation and constructive régime. Secondly, because happy social living depends upon health to some extent. The physical and the mental are so interdependent that the emotions, the moods, the temperament in fact, are largely influenced by the state of the bodily functions. Emotions in turn influence action, and so take part in habit-forming and character-building. Timely attention to impacted teeth relieved a boy of nervous irritation and helped transform him from a juvenile delinquent to a well-behaved citizen. Thirdly, unless we realize the general possibilities of the age we may make undue demands upon children's motor control, or ability to sustain attention. We may fail to make allowance for a stage of awkwardness, or for rapid fatiguability, or for a state of high tension, any of which may accompany uneven and rapid growth. If this is true for children in general it is even more true in an individual case. Knowledge of a child's health condition or of a permanent handi-cap may help to explain his vagaries, his restlessness, his moodiness, his poor adjustment in loving his neigh-bor.

FOR DISCUSSION

1. What play interests that you noted would help account for the facts as stated about death rate in this age period?

2. What proportion of the absences from Sunday school is reported as due to illness?

3. What do the facts given suggest as to the wisdom of the practice of having separate classes for boys and girls in the Junior Department?

4. Report instances of a high degree of dexterity among eleven- and twelve-year-olds.

5. What would you think of a ten-mile hike for eleven-year-old boys?

6. Ask all your pupils what time they went to bed and what time they got up, every day last week. Esti-mate the average number of hours of sleep each had, allowing one hour for the preparation for bed and lying awake.

7. How many have had tonsils or adenoids removed? How many pay regular visits to the dentist?

CHAPTER V

THE JUNIOR IN THE WORLD OF READING

Fore-Exercises

1. Ask each of your class these questions. If you have no class then try to reach six children, three boys and three girls between nine and twelve years old. (*a*) Do you take books from the public library? (*b*) If so, how often? (*c*) What was the name of your last book? (*d*) Why did you take it? (*e*) How did you like it? (*f*) If you were taken to a bookstore and told that you might choose just one book for your own, what would you select?

2. If you can, pay a visit to the public library and talk to the children's room librarian. Ask her (*a*) what magazines the children specially like, (*b*) what difference she finds between boys and girls in their reading tastes, (*c*) who are the most popular authors, (*d*) which books wear out the most quickly. Bring the results of both these exercises to class.

When Junior boys and girls are not engaged in active play—when an unwonted quiet makes you wonder if they have disappeared altogether, or if they are asleep, or if unusual mischief is brewing—what are they to be found doing? This takes no long thought to answer; the chances are you will find them curled up over a book. A wonderful gift from the work of the primary grades is this ability to read. Henceforward the wonderland of literature is theirs for the simple labor of taking down a volume from the shelf. No longer are they compelled to wait upon the art of the oral story teller. No longer need they press an uncertain adult with questions for needed knowledge. No longer must they guess at most of the contents of books from such pictures as an illustrator has provided. With the key to the printed page in their possession they can now unlock the gate to the paradise of books, finding therein many a pleasant-tasting fruit.

Kinds of books.—What sort of books are they enjoying so avidly? And what is it about the books that is the real attraction? Do nine-year-olds and twelve-year-olds read the same volumes? Do boys and girls display the same tastes?

The first of these problems is the easiest to solve; for we have only to tabulate the books actually found to be favorites, and classify them, to arrive at an answer. Undoubtedly, two thirds to three fourths of all the reading Juniors do is fiction. A book means " a story" to them, in other words, something that appeals to the imagination. Practically all the reading of the nine-year-olds is of the type known to the librarian as "juveniles." Later we find history and biography added, also books of travel, of science, those descriptive of industrial processes, and last of all poetry, but in small proportion compared to the books of fiction. Miss Josephine Baldwin in asking children to vote for the books they liked best found that 2419 choices out of 3417, or about seventy per cent, were for fiction, also that 1007 different books were mentioned. Compare the results of these questions you have put to your half dozen Juniors, and see if they are not similar. Series such as the "Rover Boys," the "Twin" books, the Scout Manuals are greatly in demand. Titles frequently given by the younger children are "Black Beauty," "Alice in Wonderland," "Gulliver's Travels." Magazines frequently asked for are The American Boy, The Youth's Companion, St. Nicholas, but not any more often these specially designed for children and young people than some others catering to older tastes primarily, such as The Strand, Saturday Evening Post, All Story Magazine, The Red Book.

Roughly, then, it would look as though books of adventure were especially sought after, those with some magic or impossible element in them, some humor, stories of family, school and college life, stories also in which animals figure, stories of exploration, of war and fighting. But books of description, biography and letters, character studies, lyric poetry, essays, exhortations, are not interesting to them sometimes they are even repulsive and boring. Novels of the rapid-moving "Rupert of Hentzau" type are enjoyed for the thrills as much as for anything else; but as a rule it is only the more precocious older girls who read novels as such.

Let us analyze a little further, and see what the younger ones prefer.

Fourth-grade preferences.—If we test as to which selection in the previous year's school reader fourth-grade children remember and like best we find stories about animals, stories about children and fairy tales leading. Stories of travel, what to the adult are

humorous stories, and poetry are hardly ever mentioned. About thirty per cent of the children give as
the reason they like this, that, or the other, that it is
"true to life"; others say vaguely that it is "beautiful,"
"interesting," showing that nine- to ten-year-olds are
not very articulate critics even though they may be
very decided in their preferences.

Of course, the type of selection put into the earlier
readers was chosen by adults who, curiously enough,
are not correct judges of children's tastes. Besides,
many selections were included merely to provide drill
in word recognition and in phonetics rather than with
the supposition that they had an interest value for little
readers. Studies of the contents of the reading texts
of the early grades show that over one half of all the
selections are poetry, about twenty-two per cent fairy
tales, eight per cent fables, three per cent biography and
history stories, the same for legend and myth, eleven
per cent miscellaneous stories, the remainder a scatter-
ing of nature study, geographical information and Bible
stories. But even though various series of readers
provide the same general class of reading matter, very
few of them include the *same* stories, or fables, or even
the same Mother Goose rhymes, showing that there has
been very little agreement as to what actual selections
are valuable as literary experiences for young children.
In an exhaustive cataloguing of twenty-two complete
series of readers containing 4,000 titles altogether,
2,500 of these occurred only once. Just twelve titles
were found in common in as many as two thirds of the
readers indexed.

So far as school training is concerned, then, it will depend on what series of readers is in use in the particular school a child attends, as to how his reading tastes have been formed by the time he is nine years old. And do not let us forget that the school training is all the reading experience some children have. Since 1905, at least, there has been very little in any school reader of a purely informational character, either of nature study, easy science, geography and history, and next to nothing suggesting things children could make or could play at, or could do. It has been assumed, whether justifiably or not, that metric verse and stories would be interesting to young children; so almost nothing else has been included in the last fifteen years or more except these two classes of material.

The second problem suggested above, namely, what are the elements which will prove the real attraction, deserves more careful consideration. Obviously, if children vote that they like a story because it is "nice," we cannot tell whether the preference is due to the presence in it of a decided plot, or of repetition, or of liveliness, or of surprise, or whether with or without much of a plot because it was about children, or animals, or magic. Miss Fannie Dunn, by means of a technical procedure, too intricate in its details to be described here, has succeeded in isolating several factors entering into stories children said they liked. Instead of considering simply the general interest, twenty different contributing factors were analyzed, for instance, fancifulness, plot, surprise, direct conversation, humor, liveliness, verse form, familiar experience, and so on. In addition, she has been able to find which elements appeal to boys of nine and ten, and which to girls. Unquestionably, stories which have surprise, and which have a definite plot, are liked. Apparently, also, "narrativeness" and liveliness are important constituents. Stories with animal or children heroes are attractive; but a narrative without these other elements fails of effect, and liveliness in itself is not a vital factor, it must be linked with plot and surprise. Boys of nine like stories with either adults or child characters as heroes, and very decidedly demand a plot in the tale. Girls are less fond of animal stories than boys, but are more keen on details that recall their own experience in home life; they like stories about girl characters. Boys rather dislike much direct conversation reported, whereas it seems a matter of indifference to girls. For both boys and girls, "moralness" has no effect one way or the other. Neither boys or girls at this age like poetry for either the elements of verse form or for that vague thing called poeticalness; poetry, in fact, seems rather repellent to them. So does also the kind of humor adults enjoy. After all, to appreciate humor means that one is able to see the fitness of things, to see the relationships in some abstract way, very often, so as to recognize the presence of the peculiar incongruity in that relationship which is termed amusing, witty, ludicrous, and so forth. Since children see relationships in only a piecemeal fashion it follows that the higher type of humor cannot be grasped by them. While they see only the big, crude outlines of relationships rather than the fine details, it follows that only humor of the broadest type will appeal. As they have but dim comprehension of abstractions, it follows that a situation, to seem funny to them, must be concrete. Thus, an erstwhile dignified person comporting himself violently as he chases a wind-blown hat, or loses his balance on an icy sidewalk is comic to them; but the finer points in a narrative are unintelligible, and consequently tiresome. Notice the slapstick comedy at which they laugh in the moving-picture houses, and the reluctance and uncertainty with which they join in the adult's appreciation of some fine points of a joke. Thus, ordinary adults' judgments of what will prove amusing for boys and girls in the first and second years of the Junior Department are likely to be quite wrong. Experiment proves, in fact, that such judgments are of little value, even in the case of experienced teachers. The only way to find out is to take the children's own testimony.

Some of these results should make us wary in selecting stories to tell our younger Junior children. Evidently we may fail to estimate aright the true interest value of a tale. Some features owe their significance to the fact that they are interwoven with other very positive attractions. A bit of verse may be a favorite because it has a good plot, and is about animals. The apparently humorous selection may be enjoyed because it has elements of surprise, and deals with child characters. The missionary talk may fail to hold attention because it is lengthy, generalized description without any semblance of a plot, or because it points a moral without being relieved by liveliness. The girls may react favorably when a story deals with familiar home experiences, whereas the boys are bored since it lacks adventure and reports much conversation.

Younger and older Juniors.—Fairy stories are a delightful prod to girls' imaginations up to about ten years old, though most boys have satisfied their desire for the miraculous and the impossible from different sources by at least nine. For both, there is a much better sense of time after ten years old. That is to say, whereas a Primary child cannot grasp the fact of centuries intervening between baby Moses and Baby Jesus, and accepts stories of Elijah and of George Washington equally as happening "once upon a time," usually after ten the stretches of the past begin to take on a perspective, so that characters and events are apprehended in better time relationship. So we find that history is read more for the chronological sequence than for the collection of tales it has been heretofore. Greek heroes are realized as dating further back than the knights of the Round Table, who again antedate the crusaders, or the early settlers of Virginia. To be sure, political and industrial developments are not grasped—people and their ways are just interestingly different. Perhaps Cæsar should have taken a train over the Alps, and the Pilgrim Fathers evidently never thought of cabling their arrival. But pity for their backwardness is swallowed up in admiration for the hero who had adventures. Daniel Boone, Robin Hood, Lincoln, Joshua, David, catch the fancy because of what they did rather than for what they were as noble characters. At this period in the fifth, sixth and seventh grades children are studying history in school; and a wise teacher will so collaborate with the town librarian that the latter has ready in tempting display historical tales that will help vivify and enlarge the background. It is now that most boys and girls make acquaintance with Fenimore Cooper and Walter Scott. Joseph Altscheler's titles, such as "The Border Watch," "Hunters of the Hills," "Masters of the Peaks," "Scouts of the Valley," "The Last of the Chiefs," and, more recently, "Guns of Europe," bear witness to the historical setting as well as to the outdoor adventure which explains in part the fascination of his books. The tendency to worship as hero the big, strong boy, shows also why stories of boy prowess at school and college athletics are such favorites in spite of—to the adult woman—endless technical detail of who got which ball, where it went and who caught it. Ask your older Juniors if they have read Heyliger's "Bucking the Line," "Against Odds," "Captain of the Nine," et cetera, and see what sort of enthusiasm you will arouse. Girls are interested in boys' stories too, but also in stories about girls, and girl life in boarding school; but boys would howl with derision at the suggestion that they read a girl's book.

Tales of battle, murder, and sudden death are exciting. The torture chambers of the Inquisition are alluring rather than revolting. There is much poring over grisly details of carnage and cruelty, a real exultation and thrill at gruesome horrors rather than any shrinking from picturing the suffering involved. The sympathetic imagination is with the active, not the passive participant in these scenes, with a vivid joy in the

power portrayed. It is not, as might be supposed, a
morbid fancy, except in rare cases.

Another interest stimulated somewhat by the subject
matter of the school curriculum is that of geography,
in the sense of this earth as man's home. Child life
of to-day in other lands, as described in the various
books of the "Twins" series by Lucy Fitch Perkins, is
fascinating to children of the fourth and fifth grades.
More of the older girls than boys read these, the latter
preferring tales of pirates, treasure seekers, pioneers,
explorers, in their enlarged idea of varied world activities.

Among other changes after ten or eleven we find a
slow-growing liking for some of the poetry of Whittier,
Longfellow, Eugene Field, James Whitcomb Riley, and
Robert Louis Stevenson. There again, it is rare to find
a child reading even narrative poetry unless directly
stimulated thereto by the experiences of school. Plays
are asked for in the library, such as they could use in
their own dramatic enterprises, rather than drama for
its own sake. "Pieces to speak" are also in demand,
since declamations are frequently included in the cele-
bration of festivals. Girls are more likely than boys to
choose verse for these occasions, while the latter may
want heroic speeches to use in character. Requests for
collections of conundrums, puns, mystery writings, code
systems, evidence the greatly increased interest in language, which enables them to appreciate plays upon
words and puzzles.

Other sex differences.—It is noticeable that boys
of eleven and twelve read with avidity such magazines

as Popular Mechanics, whereas girls seldom, if ever, find that sort of thing attractive. Boys' constructive activities run more to carpentry, girls' to sewing. The young experimenter with wireless, with dynamics, suction pumps, pulleys, levers and so forth, is, ninety-nine times out of a hundred, a boy and not a girl; so, naturally, books and papers which will explain, describe, suggest or inspire are very welcome and are eagerly sought for. Descriptions of industrial processes are read more by older boys than by older girls, unless both are required to study about them in connection with some school project. Girls read less history, on the whole, preferring the history story. Toward the end of the Junior period some few girls no longer object to the love element as a finale to a story. They no longer dismiss the courtship and proposal as the stereotyped ending to a fairy tale where the hero weds the princess and both "live happily ever after," but begin to thrill to more details for the sake of the romance in itself. Indeed, some more mature-minded girls ask for love stories and novels at twelve years of age, and do not a little inventing of their own along those lines.

Guiding these interests. — One function the Sunday-school library—if such exists—can serve, is not only to supply teachers and pupils alike with books of reference, but to do constructive work along the line of forming the taste in reading of the lighter kind. To do this, we must undoubtedly take account of the elements in fiction that are naturally appealing at this age, and then see that the trashier sort of books which appeal in a cheap way and lead on to nothing further find no place on the shelves. Those we include must possess the thrill of adventure, or deal with situations in family and school life, or introduce the reader to other lands and other times, or foster the interest in birds and animals and love of nature generally. The ideals actuating the characters are better expressed by what they do than by moralizing about them. Authors that have stood the test, are such as Alcott, Ewing, Hawthorne, Kipling, Kingsley, Malory, Mark Twain, Ruskin, Sewell, Stevenson, Jules Verne. For current fiction it would be wise to apply for an approved list to such places as your denominational headquarters, or to the Federation of Child Study with its head office in New York City, but with local chapters in several other cities. A committee publishes annually a list of new books which it would recommend for children's reading. Besides these, fairy tales for the younger ones, source books of information for the questing young scientist and the aspiring artisan must find room. "The Child's Book of Knowledge" alone would be a much beloved storehouse.

FOR DISCUSSION

1. Would Juniors be interested in the story of Esther? If so, what are the elements in it that probably make the appeal?

2. Which of each pair of characters would be more attractive to Juniors? Why? Isaac or Jacob; Ezra or Nehemiah; Peter or John; Cromwell or William Penn; William Carey or Adoniram Judson.

3. What is it about the life of David that Juniors enjoy?

4. What incidents in the life of Paul would be appealing to third and fourth year Juniors?

5. What is the best way to find out if your judgment in answering the above is good?

6. Ten-year-old Dorothy was found deep in Milton's "Paradise Lost." What do you think was the interest in it for her?

7. Eleven-year-old Randolph has read four out of five volumes of general history in his father's library. Is that unusual? Can you match that by another instance?

8. Next time Juniors are inattentive when a "talk" is being given, try to analyze the story or talk to see what elements it lacks which Juniors like, and what it over-emphasizes which they do not appreciate.

9. Study the method by which your lesson system presents the life of Christ to Juniors, compared with the way it presents the same to Intermediates. Why the difference? Do you think the emphasis is put on those things which Juniors naturally appreciate?

CHAPTER VI

NEW CAPACITY FOR DECISION

FORE-EXERCISES

1. Write down what you consider the characteristics of a "weak-willed" person—of a "strong-willed" person. Bring the list of characteristics to class and compare with what others have written. How far do the lists agree?

2. Do you think the stubborn, obstinate child of four or five will develop into a strong or a weak individual volitionally?

Independence, initiative, or self-will?—Why is it that to the popular mind the very personification of impishness, defiance and deviltry generally is to be found in the ten-or eleven-year-old boy? Why is it that authors and caricaturists alike use him as a symbol for trouble maker, and mischievous law breaker? Is there any justification for so widespread an opinion? And is the boy at this time so very different from the girl that he alone deserves these epithets? There is some foundation for this prevalent opinion. Let us see what are some of the detailed reasons therefor.

As was indicated in Chapter III, children are much more independent, physically at least, of home ties at this age than ever before. If need be they can procure food and shelter for themselves, by primitive methods, so that even for these necessities home is not absolutely indispensable. As the horizon of possibility widens, the doings and the sayings of others of like age become increasingly potent in shaping the conduct and the thinking of the individual boy and girl. In the gang or the set the restlessness of one member finds an echo. Manners called bad in the family circle are the common mode of this group. Impulses to noisiness, to fighting for one's own, to lawlessness in general are more or less restrained in the home; but they find free expression when joined to similar desires felt by the rest of the crowd, so that the mob dares to do what the individual might hesitate to undertake.

And what are some of these impulses? To quote from Joseph Lee:[1] "There is the great commandment . . . Thou shalt assert thyself. The child's creative life . . . has boiled up to the surface . . . and set forth upon the conquest of the world." He must somehow be a cause, of noise assuredly, of having things happen, of making things move, of getting other people to react in sudden and forceful ways, if comic, so much the better. If these desires make trouble for older folks, it surely is not the child's fault. Why do grownups find so many, many things inconvenient or tiresome, and why do they label these things as wrong? Let us remember, too, that the Junior's sense of ownership, or of property rights, is but rudimentary; that in this boiling over into action of his creative life many objects must be experimented with, regardless of who lays claim to possession of the said objects.

Further, let us remember that this is a healthy, al-

[1] "Play in Education." Page 239.

most rudely healthy period of childhood, the weaknesses of the earlier period outgrown, the crises of adolescence not yet at hand. With increasing vitality and endurance and great immunity from disease, a child must find outlet for the surge of physical well-being within. He must do and dare, he must spend long hours in the swimming hole, he must climb the parapet of the bridge, swing off the higher boughs of the tree, coast down the roughest slide available. Is there danger in these activities? So much the better—it is more of a sport and calls for so much more chance of self-assertion against difficulty. Is there a prohibition socially? So much the more exciting and lively does the issue become. There will be the delight of measuring wits, of inciting pursuit, of evading detection, the only shame being to be found out or to be so slow that one is caught. And since others of like mind are engaged in the same pursuits it is evident that not only will the fun be fast and furious, it will also be highly competitive. In the mutual boiling and seething of the group some one must come to the top. He who thus wins his way does it by force, not of ethical beauty, but of sheer power of domination, even to fighting every other boy who aspires to authority.

Above all, leader and followers alike must be valiant in the fray, quick with taunts and fists, ready in self-defense and pleasantly aggressive likewise. Both danger and pain must be held of little account. He who for these causes shrinks from difficult enterprise quickly finds a choice before him of facing them, or of facing the danger of contempt and the pain of jeers.

Cowardice is a fault most scorned; and the child who exhibits timidity is usually most unmercifully scoffed at and teased, frequently becoming an outcast from his kind, forced to fall back on the society of younger children.

Girls are less aggressive in their fighting, and possibly weaker in self-assertion. They are also slower than their brothers to organize effortful activity in their own sex group, though they may be just as clannish in wishing to get together. Whether from original nature or from conventional training they stay at home more, and explore abroad less than boys. Thus their mischief seems of the less overt, violent sort, and certainly does not get them into trouble with public authorities nearly so often as is the case with boys. It is, however, an age of tomboyism, when acrobatic feats are the order of the day and rivalry is very keen. Outdoor life and competitive games are alluring to the "weaker sex" too, and provide their own opportunities for planning and deciding, for finding one's own level among companions, for proving one's mettle at sports.

Social will-training.—Now in what way do these tendencies help develop the power of deciding, or what we call will power? First of all, in the hazard of the exploit and in the rapid pace of the game there arise countless necessities for deciding and acting. Indeed, he who hesitates is lost, or else loses the game and is so informed in no soft and gentle terms by the rest. Many a dawdler has found himself compelled to quick thinking and swift action by the imminence of danger or the vicissitudes of the ball game. Then again, there is the burden of sharing decisions with the rest of the group. To quote once more from Lee[1]: "There is no more prolific source of legislation than athletic competition, and no relation in life calls for a more constant exercise of the judicial faculty." In the endless stunts and competitions there is perpetual need for deciding who won, who was caught, who is out, whether so-and-so played fair. From minute to minute effort must be judged, standards must be recognized, disputes must be thrashed out, opinion must clash with opinion, and either justify itself or be converted by the majority ruling. Then, too, each must find out when to submit and when to stand up for his rights. Individual antagonisms must give way to coöperation, or wild anarchy will prevail which, in the long run, is found distinctly uncomfortable. Thus both physically and socially the power of deciding is being trained.

Decision as a habit.—The capacity for decision is developed, like any other capacity, by exercise, and by discriminative exercise on higher planes or in wider fields. Thrown on his own resources in a world of boys and girls, a child learns to hold his own by normal strength and daring. In the realm of games and play he finds his greatest social realization, and so his chief need of moral adjustment, since morality develops from social contacts. His habits of decision are needed in concrete physical situations, also in regulating the activities of the group of which he finds himself a member. He decides less by abstract ideals than by standards wrought out in the hard give and take of group

[1] "Play in Education." Page 329.

play. Hence the child who is naturally quick and firm in choosing one side of a problem often comes to be a leader, while the child who wavers may lapse into having his decisions made for him. So, too, the child who is inferior in physical prowess may learn to win his way by guile, or by tricks of "blarney," or by being shut out of many competitive games and thus missing an important form of training in decision, he may remain deficient in will power all his life.

If we analyze volition, we see that a good power of deciding implies: (1) Waiting to accumulate all the evidence before making a decision, a habit rather foreign to the impulsive Junior. (2) Refraining from a dawdling decision, a relatively easy matter at this age except in special cases. (3) Persistence in a course of action once decided on, even though it prove rather unpleasant. This is usually well disciplined by most of the activities natural to the period, but in set tasks it often needs much encouragement. Good volition also presupposes (4) ability to analyze a problem so as to choose the best course wisely, which ability at this age is of course in but an early stage of development. It is here that we can help children to think more clearly into the issues involved, and forecast the results, or retrace from effect to cause so as to judge whether or not a decision was a wise one. It also, (5) from the standpoint of character, implies the direction of conduct in accordance with ideals. These, we have seen, are seldom abstract at this age, so that the question of who is the concrete embodiment of ideals becomes very important.

The power of self-control is, of course, involved in the matter of volition. Mere impulsive action is one of the lowest forms of mental activity, the kind we expect from animals, babies, and other immature creatures. To be "disciplined," however, implies that all impulses are not immediately carried over into action, but that time is taken for deliberation. Recall and foresight will mean that some impulses are restrained and others given free rein, according to the standards felt. As children become better able to think, their possibilities of recalling and judging improve. As they actually experience the results of action, and remember these results, they will gain in foresight. As they are given opportunity to choose and decide for themselves, they gain in power to do so quickly with less effort, and with self-reliance. If they have been compelled to abide by the consequences of those decisions, whether pleasant or unpleasant, they learn to choose wisely. It follows, then, that as the time sense and memory are better in the Junior period than before, these two factors alone will contribute to increased power of decision. But real discipline will have been obtained only as the home and social training has afforded opportunity to choose, as it has discouraged vacillation or hesitation, and as it has emphasized the value of effort in sticking to a course once chosen.

In the schoolroom where the project method of teaching is used, very much more opportunity is given the child for initiating activities. He is also called on far more frequently to exercise judgment, to weigh and balance factors which should guide decisions, to plan out work and to criticize not only outcome, but efforts. An interesting thing about this method is that adults are perpetually surprised by the sensible way in which youngsters take a comprehensive view of the situation and rise to the responsibilities placed upon them. A Junior superintendent, much concerned with the apparent failure of some schemes on foot, called the eleven-year-old president of the group in consultation. To her surprise he had recognized every difficulty which she had noted, spoke of one or two more, and in addition suggested a couple of changes in policy which proved most effective. Thus, criticism can be not only unsparing at times, but it can also be constructive. The viewpoint from inside boyhood may give the angle of vision lost to the adult, and from which the way may be seen to the solution of a problem in conduct.

Home influence in will-training.—How does the home foster habits of decision? Precisely in the same way as already suggested: (1) By making opportunities for decision, in other words by giving responsibility; (2) by allowing the results of decision to be felt, criticizing in the light of the pleasantness or unpleasantness of the results; (3) by making lack of decision, and too hasty decision, uncomfortable; (4) by insisting on self-control.

A home where there is little or no routine, where a vacillating policy and the whim of the moment are all that determine the elders' movements, offers little that is good will-training to the growing child. He has no standard to imitate beyond that of seeking his own immediate convenience and bids fair to develop into an undisciplined, selfish, tyrannical adult. On the other hand, a home where everything is reduced to a military routine, which permits no individual choice in any matter, so mechanizes a child that when he is later thrown on his own responsibility in a different environment, he seems at a loss to know what to do. The happy medium is, of course, not too easy to acquire, especially when so much depends on the different temperaments of the members of the household as well as on their number. Some routine there must be; but instead of blindly following it, children must be led to intelligent coöperation therein. There is not only the regulation to be obeyed, but also the necessity of understanding the purpose of that regulation. As we have seen, children feel the force of a rule in a game when they themselves have helped formulate it. Consequently, in many matters of home life, such as the times to do certain tasks, the places where things are to be kept, waiting upon oneself rather than demanding service from others, planning help for the others, planning ways of entertaining, children must be habituated to consider the advisability of this or that course, choose one, and thereafter stick to the choice.

The same principles of habit-forming (exercise and reward) apply here as elsewhere. Given the interest and motive to plan and choose, they must have such choices with some frequency, feel the effects with full force whether agreeable or disagreeable, and take time for criticism and appreciation of the wisdom of their choice. Only so can worthy responsibility grow.

Compare these treatments of children. Raymond's

mother calls, "Now, dear, go and wash your hands, it's nearly supper time," in such a tone that all the response she gets is, "Uh huh." Five minutes later it is "Raymond, didn't you hear mother ask you to wash your hands? Well, please go and do as I ask you." "All right, in just a minute." Two minutes later, "Raymond, do go, here's supper just ready, and I asked you before." Scramble from the boy, irritation for mother. Yet Raymond himself says, "When Miss Forrest says, 'Now, children, you have just fifteen minutes to do that,' I know I have just that time and then it's got to be ready." Of course, the mistake was made long before, in Raymond's training. Compare his father's method, when he is called in to supplement authority. He demands, "Well sir, am I going to be obeyed or not? Go do what you're told at once"—and gets obedience, of a kind. Compare the home where the children are held responsible for knowing not only supper time, but also five minutes beforehand that they must get ready; also that without being reminded by anyone else, when the clock indicates the bedtime agreed upon, bedwards they must start.

A vacillating, dawdling child frequently becomes upset and nervous if pressure is brought to bear from the outside to make better speed; but by suffering the social consequences of dilatoriness, losing a treat, missing a privilege, getting no choice at all because of slow action, he will be more likely to apply the pressure himself from the inside, and so learn the value of quicker decisions.

Persistence in sticking to a task until finished is one

of the most difficult traits to train. The lack of it is
more surely a sign of a weak will than manner of
choice is, since choices are often made through impulse,
whereas plodding to the end often goes against impulse
and demands effort. Here too is where too soft-
hearted (or is it soft-headed?) parents are apt to
weaken, to feel sorry for the child who is feeling discomfort in his effort, and to finish the task for him, or
condole with him and excuse the completion altogether.
A more "penny wise, pound foolish" plan could not be
imagined. They are not only not helping the child form
habits of perseverance, but they are deliberately forming habits in him of setting present pleasure highest, of
doing scamped work, forming the kind of character no
one can trust. Far better to experience both the present
discomfort and the permanent worth. An appeal to
honor can be made here, as a motive for the habit of
sticking to it.

Emotional self-control must be fostered in every
way, according to the tendencies of the particular child.
Again the laws of habit-forming apply. Motivate for
self-control, reward when it is well done, make the lack
of it disagreeable.

Our part in training the will.—Since it is only by
exercise that a capacity can grow we must see to it that
no child, no group, is so sheltered from crises demanding thought, so dictated to whenever a question of behavior arises, that no chance of planning and deciding
is afforded. Moreover, we need to see that they feel
the consequences of their decisions so as to be better
judges next time. We must emphasize the connection

between the happy results and the wise choice. We must not weakly nullify the results of an unwise choice, but let them learn from the ensuing discomfort not to make that particular kind of error again.

Indications of a faultily trained will are to be found in fits of sulkiness or fits of obstinacy. The former is a weak, helpless way of meeting the unpleasantness of being thwarted, instead of the more efficient thinking which discovers some other way out of the discomfort. The latter, obstinacy, is of two kinds: (1) positive—persistent effort in the face of social prohibition, or (2) negative—refusal to comply with a request. The positive kind is misdirected attention, and needs treatment by distraction, by substituting some other equally attractive occupation. The negative is due to a species of paralysis, and inability to act, rather than a genuine refusal. To leave such cases alone is wiser than to try to force the issue, until the "cold lump inside" has melted. Friendly sympathy or the warmth of humor, after a judicious interval of letting alone, will often hasten this melting process. In any case, a conflict of wills should be avoided as far as possible. If the adult conquers the child, our real goal—that of self-mastery has not been attained. If the child wins over the adult it establishes a bad precedent. In either case an ugly scar is left in consciousness.

How then is self-mastery attained? From the beginning of life every impulse to act is provided with complementary counterchecks. As one muscle contracts another relaxes, to render possible the total movement of raising and bending the arm, for instance.

The impulse to touch the flame is inhibited by the impulse to draw away as the excessive heat is felt. The impulse to give way to anger is checked by the recollection of how badly some one's feelings were hurt last time. The fear of balancing alone on the high, narrow plank is outweighed by the fear of being laughed at if one hangs back. The desire to eat candy now is balanced by the desire to keep some to share with a chum. The thought of spending all one's money on a coveted object is met by the thought of saving some for a greater necessity, and so on. Again it is the grasp of consequences that stimulates the memory, and trains the judgment. A well-balanced, self-controlled child is one who is so coördinating his antagonistic impulses that they no longer conflict, but work together as do the muscles of his arm in throwing a ball.

What to expect.—Are there any standards by which to measure a child and see whether or not he is up to normal for his age in power of self-control? Not yet, as derived from scientific experiment, in any such definite way as to enable us to determine degree of development physically and mentally. There is a good consensus of opinion from parents and educators, to be sure; but we still await the type of character test necessary to determine a child's status volitionally for his age. Here are a few suggestions for the home. By nine years old a child can be held responsible for keeping his toys and his clothes in their assigned places, for consulting the weather and the thermometer to know —as previously discussed and agreed upon—what outer clothing will be necessary. By eleven a child should be able to select a meal wisely and economically from the restaurant bill of fare. By twelve a self-reliant child should be able to take tickets, check trunks, consult time-tables and plan routes. Both eleven- and twelve-year-olds should be expected to act adequately as host or hostess to those of their own age, mapping out the entertainment, planning and helping to prepare the refreshments. Increasingly, Juniors should earn a reward before enjoying it, take "pain before pleasure" if it means choosing the relatively unattractive course first. Habits of thrift, of dependability in completing assigned tasks, of meeting appointments reliably and punctually, should be well formed in all sorts of situations, remembering that habits do not grow by exhortation from the elders, but by frequent chances to practice them.

For Discussion

1. In what way may training in obedience foster self-control?

2. How may an obedient child have missed any worth-while volitional training?

3. Why may daydreaming tend to weaken the will?

4. What has attention to do with will power?

CHAPTER VII

THE NATURE AND VALUE OF MEMORY

Fore-Exercise

If you conveniently can, ask a ten-year-old child to learn aloud for you some brief selection, say the first six verses of Psalm 19. Make it clear that you want everything out loud, the thinking and the practice and all. Do not offer any suggestions as to method, but note carefully what your subject does. For example, does he read it all through first or concentrate on memorizing it verse by verse? Does he stop over the figures of speech to get the picture mentally? Does he ask himself what the longer, possibly less familiar words mean? Does he gabble as he repeats it? Does he look off, to test whether he knows it? Take careful note of exactly what he does.

Before reading this chapter, ask yourself by what different method, if any, you would set about memorizing such a selection yourself. How would you prepare to teach such a selection to a class of children of that age?

Popular beliefs concerning children's memories.— You have doubtless often heard it said that children learn much more easily than adults do, or that childhood is the golden age for memory, or that what we learn as children we never forget, or that children have better memories than adults. Let us see how nearly true these statements are, and whether they all mean the same thing or not.

The more we study what constitutes memory the more we have to admit that it is not one thing but several, that we have not a memory, but many memories, for this, that and the other—a fact that any person will claim in self-defense when he says he has a poor memory for names, but a good memory for faces. We find, likewise, that learning in the sense of memorizing is not an identical process at all times with all people, and that remembering may mean several different things depending on the connection in which the term is used.

Meanings of memory.—John does not remember well enough to describe the place by the brook where they had a picnic last week, but he remembers it when he sees it again. Eva remembers how she lost her hair ribbon where they scrambled through the bushes, and has a vivid visual image of the whole place. Both think that they will remember how to swim this summer; both remember a number of doggerel conundrums that they enjoy repeating. Both remember the main points in an exciting story they have read only once. In such a tangle of meanings, what kinds of memory can be distinguished?

The chief thing in common with all these rememberings is that really a habit has been called to action—a previously formed connection of thoughts, or actions, or feelings. Something is done again that has been done before but not immediately before—as in swimming, or recognizing the picnic place—or something is felt or thought of again after an interval during which other matters have occupied the attention. If the former sequence of action or thought is peculiar to the person experiencing it—as Eva's recollection of losing her ribbon—we have what has been termed memory proper. It is this thread of recollection and identification of our own life that keeps us one unitary personality through different periods. Eva remembers things she did at five years old not because she has been told about them by other people, but because she is able to bring them back with the inner, individual viewpoint; thus her memory of an event is colored differently from her mother's memory of the same, indeed from that of everyone else.

When we remember facts learned, such as a pair of names together of state and capital, we obviously do not have to invoke this personal memory, only to see to it that a habit of thinking and saying or writing these two names together persists. Teachers probably call this the most important form of memory, since it is the form they are chiefly concerned in training. Habits of skill which remain after a lapse of time also share the term memory. In this case muscles are involved; and it is interesting to note that sometimes the muscles seem to remember beautifully when we have not known beforehand whether we could still ride horseback, or swim, or play a particular selection on the piano.

Sometimes to remember something implies having now a mental image of how the original impression looked, or sounded, or felt. We can call up to the mind's eye or the mind's nose or the mind's ear some experience that formerly assailed the real eyes, nose, and ears. We may even be helped to remember music by the place on the page where it was printed, or remember what we are going to say to an audience by gesturing in imagination.

Children's memories.—Before we explore further into the meanings of memory let us get an idea of how good children of Junior age may be with these four forms of memory.

So far as memory proper, or personal memory is concerned, children will be accurate in this just in proportion as they were deeply impressed at the time of the occurrence, or were attentive to their own experience. They are rather susceptible to suggestion, so that if plied with leading questions they may be led to falsify their accounts unintentionally rather more easily than adults, but less easily at twelve than at nine. Curiously, being absolutely positive as to the details of an affair by no means indicates real reliability; it is the child who is trained to be observant and to verify particulars while still observing who tends to be accurate, not the one who is willing to swear he is right in his account. To repeat a version of an occurrence, especially several times over to sympathetic audiences, tends to fix the facts mentioned, whether they were originally correct or not; it also tends to distort the general accuracy, since stories will grow in the direction of the narrator's wishes and ambitions. Thus we should be wary in pressing children for details in conflicting accounts of a quarrel, for instance, and should particularly discount any figures of how often, how many, how long, how much, since such estimates are scarcely ever correct and are the first to suffer change by repetition.

In the next two kinds of memory, mental associations and muscle habits, children of this age have a decided advantage. Once the association is really made, granted that the facts will stick for at least twenty to thirty minutes, children retain what they learn very well indeed. There has been a steady increase in this power of retention from the earlier years, and the maximum is reached some time before fourteen, so that every year of the Junior period sees the children better able to remember, in this sense, than ever before. They can also do as well as the sixteen-year-olds by the time they are eleven or so, and better than people in the twenties, once they have really learned the material. This also holds good with many muscle memories. Some skilled habits must, indeed, be acquired in childhood because bones and muscles are so much more plastic in the early years. An acrobat must begin training before ten; a pianist or violinist labors much harder in the teens to acquire the technique that would have come easily in the previous years.

For the fourth meaning of memory, it seems probable that children's imagery is much more vivid than that of adults, who have replaced it with other aids to recall. Certainly their images of things actually seen, heard, tasted, and felt are more concrete than the cold, pale word representing the experience which is all that many adults use in the way of imagery, especially when they are thinking rapidly or in abstract terms. Not that an image helps necessarily to make the memory any more trustworthy, but it seems more interesting because of the lifelikeness of the details involved.

To sum up the facts so far:

(1) Children of Junior age may have good personal memories; but unless they are carefully attentive to an occurrence they may easily be inaccurate in narrating it.

(2) They retain facts, once well learned, better than ever before, and almost better than ever again.

(3) Many muscle habits are better formed now, (if not earlier) than later on.

(4) Their imagery is vivid and concrete, largely visual, and helps to make the memory content interesting.

Memorizing.—If we ask by what process facts come to be entrusted to memory in the first place, we find that in the main there are two methods. The first of these has to do chiefly with the original external impressions. We may repeat an impression so often that in spite of very little effort of attention the thing is learned. Thus we learn popular music or acquire information about so-and-so's commodities, because we hear the former so frequently, or because the advertisement of the latter meets our eyes at every turn. Children will start to memorize by this method, repeating a stanza or even a line of poetry many times with little or no attention as they gabble faster and faster, depending on brute repetition to drive the thing home. Unfortunately, the less the attention the more it is likely that mistakes will creep in unnoticed, and be perpetuated. Of this kind is the "practice" on the piano when the fingers go through some motions perfunctorily while the story book propped open on the rack absorbs the attention.

However, we may depend not so much on the number of original impressions as on their intensity. We may have so sensational a presentation, one appealing to the interest and the imagination, that relatively few repetitions suffice to fix the thing in mind. Or we may so concentrate and force ourselves to attend that very much less time is required, and fewer repetitions, to learn the material. Children are not so likely to force themselves unless there is some element of competition introduced, even a race against time. It is obviously more economical to learn with energy and interest than to dawdle along with inattentive repetitions; so that it pays to devise means of making vivid the appeals to children's eyes and ears, or to include dramatization or construction work that will intensify the external impressions. Moreover, since presenting material to eyes, ears, and muscles, not only makes for vividness but provides for individual differences to some extent and also allows extra repetition, we should take care to include several forms of presentation rather than simply to repeat the same form several times. Thus, they should read as well as listen to words and music, say them out loud and, after ten years old, write them also, provided the act of writing is not still so laborious that it absorbs attention in itself.

The second method on which we depend in memorizing has to do with the associations formed, with the thoughts called up and linked with the things to be learned, with the weaving together of the new, incoming material with the patterns of thought already familiar. Thus, we study the new, analyze or outline it, seeing the relationship of its parts, group it under certain classification heads, illustrate it from our previous experience, appreciate its beauty, understand it, think about it, after which the matter of memorizing the exact word sequence is quick and easy.

Of these two methods children seem to use the first—that of relying on many repetitions of the external impression—rather than really thinking out the significance of the meaning. It has been questioned, indeed, whether the fact that material had any meaning at all made any difference to them, so little attention do they seem to pay to the meaning, and so easily do they allow false interpretations to creep into their singsong, rote memorizing. Experiments were made therefore to see if they would learn nonsense as rapidly as meaningful material. It was found that after all, they did not; and, moreover, if careful heed is given to forming rich and plentiful associations instead of to emphasizing mere externals, they learn still better. It pays, then, to see that children think about and understand the hymns, passages of Scripture or whatever we ask them to memorize, from the standpoint both of rapidity of learning and of likelihood of retention.

For example, to insure association rather than brute repetition as a method of learning Psalm 121, we should first call attention to the group of psalms entitled "songs of degrees," and explain the term. Vividly, the scenery on the journey to Jerusalem might be recalled, and the dangers of travel. Further description of the value of a guide and a sentinel to whom the welfare of pilgrims is intrusted, and we have a series of rich pictures in the children's minds. Then we might ask what the people who stayed at home would wish for their friends who are bidding them goodbye. By dramatizing the two voices, and following the stanza form as printed in such a version as Moulton's, we shall get an appreciative understanding of the beautiful song that will greatly facilitate the work of mere memorization. A little attention to the sequence of words—help, keep, preserve—and a very few repetitions will suffice.

Memorizing depends not only upon the kind of associations formed but also upon the number of things the attention can grasp at once. There is a gradual enlargement in this span of attention as children get older. If we pronounce a series of numbers aloud slowly, at the rate of one per second, and ask children to write down the list after we have finished, we shall find that on the average, children of ten years can get six or seven correctly and in order, whereas the ordinary adult can give eight. The same holds true of unrelated words, nonsense syllables, abstract terms, series of tones which do not suggest a melody, series of objects shown, sounds made, and so forth. This power of immediate reproduction of impressions increases gradually all through childhood and up to about twenty-five years of age. A ten-year-old is better than an eight-year-old, but not so good as a twelve-year-old, and not nearly so good as the eighteen-year-old. In this sense of memorizing children are at a disadvantage compared with young adults. Moreover, if within ten minutes we ask children to tell us the series again without first refreshing their memory, we shall find they have forgotten far more than older boys or girls or adults in the same short period . Up to twenty minutes they forget impressions very rapidly. What sticks in mind over and beyond that length of time is apt to remain better for them than for older people, though the latter make a better showing during that twenty minutes because of better attention span to the one repetition.

To sum up again:

(5) In the process of memorizing children tend to depend on a great number of repetitions, often with little concentration and no attention to the meaning.

(6) It is more profitable to help them improve their methods of attending, and to provide for a variety of impressions than for mere frequency.

(7) It is still more profitable to develop habits of critical, appreciative learning, than to permit mere rote memorizing.

(8) After one repetition only, Juniors cannot reproduce immediately as much as adults can, and they will at first forget more rapidly than adults. Anything remembered beyond twenty minutes is likely to be retained by them better than by adults.

Still we are not done with meanings of "remember." We have discussed retention. We have considered the process of learning, but how is a thing recollected? How do we prove that we have first learned, then retained a fact? Retention only suggests that an association once formed has stayed; but how is it brought back when wanted for use? Retention is a resting state, but remembering is an active thing, after all.

Recognition and recall.—The two terms we employ are to recognize, and to recall. To recognize anything means only that we act with familiarity towards an object which is presented to us. Thus, we identify last night's burglar from the line-up of suspects, we pick out the melody we heard and liked from several that are now played over for us, we are unable to remember a person's name until it is told us once more, when we say, "Of course, that is it." You see, it is an easy form of memory which even animals develop, since they react with habits previously learned to familiar sounds, smells, places and so forth. It is set going by an immediate stimulus to the senses; for this reason, then, it is less useful for independent thinking than is recall, which means the ability to reinstate some past association in our thinking more or less fully without any present aid from outside. Many facts we once learned are not retained well enough to be recalled, though as soon as some one tells us the facts over again we are able to recognize them. Consequently we have a much wider, more inclusive field of recognition than we have of recall; and even in more definite recall this background of nearly but not quite remembered associations sets the stage, so to speak, and induces prejudice, bias, emotional sympathy or antipathy in our reactions. Thus a child may retain and recognize a feeling of dislike for some one, and show it at the next meeting too, though he can recall no specific grounds for the dislike in anything that has happened. Children are not different from adults in the use of recognition and recall except that they have to be trained to practice recall during the process of memorizing rather than to rely on such promptings and cues as will involve recognition only.

When a pupil is endeavoring to recall, one can often discover whether he learned more by impressions or by associations. If the former, then he will try to revive the original impressions in the form of imagery, or will be forced to repeat an entire word sequence from the beginning to get his cue. If he learned by association, he will now consider the meaning again, think of the argument, of the relationship of the parts, or whatever appropriate connection was made while learning, and so recall in that way.

To help train pupils to recall and to learn by association, we should suggest that when memorizing a selection, say, of thirty lines or so, they should read over the whole and find its meaning, and keep on reading the entire passage rather than attacking it a few lines at a time, piecemeal fashion. After grasping the meaning of the whole, thinking out further illustrations, appreciating the symbolism, if any, and following the progression of thought, they should read the whole rapidly several times, then test themselves to see how much they can recall. Upon discovering the weak points these can be dwelt on specially, then fitted in to the whole again.

It is better, too, for children to spend twenty to twenty-five minutes memorizing by this method, then to take a rest, then to spend fifteen minutes, then have another interval, and later on spend ten minutes in reviewing and recalling, than it would be to spend all fifty minutes in one stretch. Each study period should begin and end with attempted recall of the whole.

Individual differences in memory.—Of course, everyone remembers more easily those things in which he is interested, and children are no exception to this rule. Since children of Junior age have limited and imperfect ideas of abstractions, it follows that their memory for abstract terms is poor as compared to that for the words that remind them of concrete, visible objects. Between ten and twelve years old their ability to remember and reproduce immediately lists of numbers, or of words denoting objects or sounds increases very rapidly. After eleven years old girls are rather better at this than boys in the quantity they can recall, though they do not so often get the order exactly right. Boys do better in reporting objects seen than in repeating merely words which refer to objects. Both do poorly with words that refer to emotions, since such words are usually abstract terms. Some children with vivid fancy will remember, not so much the actual things they see and hear as the thoughts they have had concerning these experiences, or will recall other information they have associated with one given fact. Others again, with a special aptitude for statistics or for music, or for form, space and color, will develop special memories along these lines. Here too, different interests will dominate. Of two boys, both with an aptitude for figures, one becomes a walking encyclopædia on railroad matters, knowing whole time-tables in detail apparently, mileage, times of arrival and departure of scores of trains. The other can reel off batting averages of numberless baseball heroes. Two other children, both musically inclined, differ so that one easily and quickly picks up any melody she has heard two or three times and can sing it, or reproduce it on the piano, while the othe ris not satisfied until she has the right harmonization and changes of key. She sings alto in school, but never learns her part by itself, always by listening to its relationship to the soprano. "Ear-minded," both of them, you suppose! But Mary visualizes the whole harmonic chord on the keyboard, even when she is singing just one tone of it.

FOR DISCUSSION

1. How does rhythm help fix facts in children's memories?

2. Is there any advantage in learning by rote the names of the Bible books in order? What would be a better way to learn? Why?

3. State the objections from the psychological point of view to having children of ten memorize the Beatitudes.

4. Why should a child think through a selection, say Psalm 1, when memorizing, rather than begin to learn it, a verse at a time?

5. Does your church require a catechism to be learned? What difficulties have you found in teaching it? What facts stated about memory in this age period would explain the difficulties?

6. Select four hymns, the words of which you think suitable and interesting to Junior children. Plan definitely and in detail how to teach one of them.

7. Is, or is it not, a good plan to have first-year Juniors write out the Bible verse you wish them to learn?

CHAPTER VIII

HERO WORSHIP

Fore-Exercise

It is suggested that you ask the following questions of any boys or girls of Junior age of your acquaintance. The purpose is to get at their own ideas on the subject, so do not suggest any ethical standards of your own. Lead up to each question in an informal, conversational way, so that no child will suspect he is under investigation, and ask each child singly, not in the presence of the rest of the group.

(*a*) When would it be wrong for a boy not to fight? When does he just have to?

(*b*) If you could have for a chum the very nicest and best sort of person you could think of, what would he (or she) be like?

(*c*) What does it mean to be patriotic? When were you patriotic?

(*d*) Did you ever turn a boy out of your gang? What for?

(*e*) If you could be somebody else for a week, anyone you know or have read about, whom would you choose? (Ask again, if Washington, or Lincoln is given.) Why?

Feelings of worth.—Whom does the small boy admire? What sort of individual is enshrined in the heart of the girl worshiper? Some indication to this we have already had in noting the sort of character most appreciated in the books read at this period. You remember that the fiction that holds both boys and girls is the sort that deals with exciting adventures, exploration, fighting, school athletics and sports; that in addition, older boys enjoy details of workmanship, and girls like stories about other girls—boarding-school life with its descriptions of friendships, jealousies, and innocence triumphing over unjust suspicion. We saw also that though pure imaginative games are rather on the decrease, yet the individual imagination may be much preoccupied with picturing oneself performing thrilling feats.

If we analyze these characters, we find certain outstanding features in common. The ball player, the pioneer, the bandit, the sea captain, the soldier of fortune are alike in exhibiting physical prowess. They all achieve the impossible against overwhelming odds; they all prove superior to every type of opposition. Further, they are fearless, skillful in some physical technique, and, to maintain interest, they must be in courageous action practically all the time. For the weakling our Juniors have contempt rather than pity, with the timid they show impatience; at the romantic sentimentalist they hoot derision. Not without reason is this age period termed dry and hard, since there is so little responsive thrill to pure beauty as such, or to virtues such as patience, desire for truth, benevolence, or to intellectual and artistic superiority. Some years later homage to these will be paid, and also to the wonder of self-effacing love. It is not until well into the teens that interest will be felt in growth in character. Now, the hero is emphatically the doer, a "mere peg to hang adventures on," a nondescript lay figure in himself perhaps, but outwardly painted in marvelously crude, bold slashes of color.

Concrete heroes.—Besides these characters in fiction and history who satisfy the imagination, what actual people around stir them to admiration? Some heroes are carried over from an earlier period of childhood, but in a more personal, less general way. Thus, one favorite is the brakeman on the train on which a group of children ride daily to school—not just any brakeman such as the five-year-old imagines himself to be in his dramatic game, but this particular, friendly, authoritative Frank. Then again, there is the policeman at the traffic corner—not just any policeman, but just that Mr. O'Connor who pilots hundreds of children as they go to school, who greets so many by name, but is so peremptory in his commands and so implicitly obeyed. Charlie Chaplin, Houdini, the clown in the circus, the real live baseball star, these are other heroes less often seen, but known through the medium of newspaper or picture.

What is the common characteristic of these? Again it is power, manifest, physical, undoubted. At a signal or slight motion of theirs something happens, either in material objects or in the behavior of crowds. Nevertheless, he-who-must-be-obeyed, or he-who-causes-effects is not a personal hero if he is unfriendly in attitude. Gruffness that is the expression of morose surliness repels children as surely as gruffness that covers real good will proves no disguise to them, so magnetically are they drawn to the comradeship beneath.

The athlete, then, the fighter, the powerful authority

are heroes; and we should rejoice that manliness and strength, even in its cruder forms, are the qualities that appeal. Power over things is also appreciated. He-who-makes-things-happen, and he-who-produces-effects wins respectful attention. Penetrate to the center of attraction of a crowd of boys, and you will find them absorbed in watching some such processes as mixing concrete, repairing machinery, or even merely changing the landscape by digging. The craftsman, then, holds second rank as hero.

But apart from these types of adults, the one who really excites the most direct, yet blind worship from ten- to twelve-year-old boys is, interestingly enough, some boy three or four years older who is a leader not of their gang, but of his own age group. Him the youngsters not so much like as follow and serve, if permitted, with dog-like devotion, though he prefers to mix with his own kind and seldom tolerates their company very long. From this lordly being a hint is more effective than a long exhortation from an adult often is. Should he require some one to go on an errand half a dozen of them will be tumbling over each other to render service. Should he graciously dispense favors they will bask in the grateful sunshine. Should he loftily disdain their presence or their toadying, they will creep to the miserable banishment he decrees. And as imitation is the sincerest form of flattery, so does their intense admiration lead them to copy their hero's gestures, his intonation, his slang, his chosen swear-words. His gait, his manner of pitching ball, his postures are so faithfully reproduced that by carefully observing a younger boy the model can often be guessed.

How all-important it is, then, that the habits of the idolized one should be sufficiently good to copy, that his ideals and voiced opinions should be worth adopting! His influence is so potent over these younger boys that, if it be a desirable one, the problem of training these Juniors is well on the way to be solved. So true is this that in the old established boys' schools the most effort is spent upon instilling the right ideals into these fourteen- to sixteen-year-old boys, knowing that they in turn will set the tone, will pass on the ancient traditions to the younger ones, and exact from them the best behavior in accord therewith. Even in a family the same thing is frequently seen between brothers four years or so apart in age.

Besides this chief danger in hero worship, that the hero may be unworthy of imitation—a clear case of misplaced trust and the establishment of bad habits— there are dangers for the worshipers in the reaction of their own attitudes upon themselves, though not nearly as serious now as in the teen age to follow. One is lest the emotional, sentimental side be developed at the expense of clear vision. Not particularly strong in critical analysis in any case, they may be so dazzled by the hero that they fail to discriminate in any way, admiring everything about him, dross and gold alike. Thus, distorted ideas of worth may influence their thinking and their actions for too long. If the idol is suddenly revealed to have clay feet, the shock of disillusionment seems too great to be borne. More often they gradually outgrow the attitude, or replace the idol with another, so to speak. Another danger is that their behavior may be erratic to the point of being ridiculous. With the overromantic attachment particularly, this is likely to be true. A sickly sentimentalism prompts social conduct that is embarrassing to the idolized one, and a bad precedent for good manners now, and self-control in love affairs later. In severe cases tasks are neglected while the worshiper loiters, longing for attention, or performing any kind of queer antics merely to get noticed.

Another danger is that the sense of loyalty to either hero or group—to be discussed later—may be misdirected so that secrecy is maintained at the wrong time. Rather than betray their friend or their gang, children will be silent when timely information would bring much needed help. Dislike of telling tales so colors their interpretation of the seriousness of a situation that evils may go unchecked and the morals of the group be imperiled.

Girls' admirations.—The same sort of hero in fiction appeals to girls, as well as the public character vested with power. When it comes to patterning themselves after some contemporary model they, too, may become volunteer feudal retainers of an older member of their sex. This overlord may be an adolescent girl, but is quite as likely to be a much older woman. Her the eleven-year-olds adore. To hear her adversely criticized is acute suffering to them, so blindly and romantically are they devoted. But though blind, girls are not nearly so inarticulate as boys. Where both are led to seek the company of the adored one, boys often express their chivalry by action only, and compensate for courteous, helpful deeds by a studied ungraciousness of manner and speech. Not for worlds would they risk being called "teacher's pet," for instance. Girls, on the contrary, are more ready with protestations of affection, with attempted caresses, and may be addicted to fetishism in treasuring mere belongings of the beloved being. The relationship sought is more personal with girls, and more exclusive too, so that girls oftener than boys suffer attacks of jealousy or morbid brooding when some other girl seems to win favor. Where boys will serve contentedly in a group, and when summarily dismissed fall back on each other's company, girls will compete for privileges, and bear discomfiture alone.

Group loyalty.—Herein lies the secret of the different ways in which boys and girls develop at this time. They arrive at self-realization by somewhat different means, due to the relative strength in them of certain instincts. From eleven on has been termed the age of loyalty by Joseph Lee. This is partly because a strong desire to "belong" drives from 75 to 90 per cent of boys between eleven and fifteen to be part of a gang, in which loyalty is the chief virtue. From eight years old, indeed, boys are more obviously gregarious than girls, and manifest a greater desire to foregather with their kind. There is no definite plan at first, certainly no real organization in the sense of selecting members or officers, just a drifting together of boys of like age in the same neighborhood as simply as the herding of cows or sheep, and as irresistibly as the attracting and coalescing of the bubbles in your teacup. Having come together, they may or may not find congenial occupation of a worth-while sort, and they are easily at the mercy of whatever impulses the more forceful spirits among them may feel. In the process of finding their own level, socially, the natural leader comes to the top and dominates the rest. This may be because his suggestions prove interesting, or because he wins dominion by the primitive means of fighting it out. He may hold his place until another boy forces his way up and upsets the balance of power; or he may be the chief in one field of action while another is the leader in some other sphere where he is superior. Such natural groups include six to eight boys as a rule, less often a dozen, rarely enlarging to as many as twenty. Gradually the group consciousness emerges until at ten years old the gang feels the need of a name by which to refer to itself. The Tough Kids, the Dowser Glums, the Wild Indians, the Wharf Rats, the Moonlight Howlers, the Red Devils, the Egg Men, the Sluggers are samples of appellations which give some index to the aspirations, if not to the activities of the gang. More titles are derived from the locality where most of the members live, just as our national names of Danes, Romans, Mexicans are used. Individual members are known to each other by some nickname, bestowed generally by reason of its descriptive appropriateness. Pug, Frenchie, Red, explain themselves; Twister refers to ball-pitching ability.

With the name, a habitation is needed to express the group idea. Either they preëmpt some special spot as a meeting ground to which no other gang may lay claim, or if opportunity offers they erect their own "hang out," be it a shanty in the woods, or a shelter in some vacant city lot painstakingly constructed from old boxes, matting, discarded linoleum, and any other handy waste material. Here the tribe makes its headquarters, sits in solemn conclave, and delights in cooking such provisions as its members can acquire for that perennial hungry feeling. The gang may sometimes adopt a distinguishing badge, and arrange initiations for would-be members. More often they just wait and try out the new boy, letting him belong, as he so craves to do, if he proves a "good fellow." This implies, first and foremost, that he is no coward, no telltale, and that he will stick by the gang. They may have few or no rules; but the boy who sneaks, or in any way betrays the gang to its natural foes is put out of the gang as inevitably as boys are boys. Thus, the first and great virtue is loyalty, developed as far as the group consciousness extends.

Common ends and purposes.—Much might be said of the natural activities of the gang. These surely must satisfy the restlessness of the age and provide continual excitement. Just what form this excitement will take depends somewhat on the social status of the boys composing the group, the ideals in the homes from which they come, and the special interests of the leader. Some groups spend all their time together in athletics of some sort, and all groups include games some of the time. Adventures are sought by land and water, not to mention fire. Fights with other gangs are a common occurrence, indeed a necessity at some stage or other. The long tramp with picnic meals, the rides stolen on freight cars, the days spent on hunting or fishing expeditions, testify to the strength of the migratory tendency. Devices to plague people "to get the chase" show the hunting impulse in another form. Raids on orchards, petty larceny of edibles of all kinds, thefts of junk, illustrate the predatory instincts. These five forms of activity are the most frequent—athletics and games, fighting, wandering afield, plaguing people and stealing. Obviously, some of them are extremely likely to get boys into trouble socially. Yet in the sequent conflict with authority the loyalty of the gang is proved in that its members escape or suffer as a body, but find it unthinkable for one to save himself at the expense of the rest.

Loyalty is felt also for members of the family, the social unit in which the boys have functioned earlier. Boasting and bragging of father's and brother's prowess is a familiar form in which this shows, also the fact that no boy will tolerate insulting remarks about his mother.

Working out, too, from the sense of belonging to a certain locality we find an incipient loyalty to the neighborhood, the school, the small town, intensified to consciousness by the latent hostility felt for boys from other neighborhoods, other schools, other towns. Just here is the contact we need to transform the narrow loyalty to the small group into the wider loyalty to the large group. If we do not want to foster the prejudiced loyalty in adult life which is merely an enlarged selfishness, we must see to it that boys do not suffer from arrested development at this stage. Their small unit must be one of several coequal units integrated into a larger whole, just as our local societies are but branches of a state or nation-wide organization. Their grade in school is thus merged into the whole school, and is not sufficient unto itself; the school again is but a part of the town, county, and eventually State system. So their small gang must articulate, or federate, if we want to widen the horizon to make room for the growing social self.

Girls' groups.—Girls, as already stated, are more personal in their relationships than boys. A frequent necessity is one special chum, to whom they early promise to tell everything, from whom they will have no secrets, and whose secrets, in turn, they will never, never tell. Alas, when the six to ten months' special attraction is over, a girl seldom feels the obligation of keeping that chum's confidences inviolate, and gives as sufficient explanation of a betrayal, "Oh, but I'm not friends with her any more." They play in groups and like to feel they "belong" with the older girls, but the group consciousness as such does not crystallize into anything very definite or very long-lived. After ten years old we are more apt to find them forming sets, cliques, or clubs, the chief charm of which is the exclusiveness which spells secrecy. Even so, the bonds which unite them seem less tough in fiber, the identification of the individual's interests with those of the group is less complete than is the case with boys. Their loyalty is weaker, and consequently needs very careful fostering. The activities of their groups are far less often athletic, and scarcely ever include fighting and raiding. Adventure is welcome, but girls seldom go so far from home and do such daring things in a group, as boys do. The club for the club's sake, just for the fun of having a secret society, is the thing five times as often as with boys, according to Sheldon's statistics; clubs are formed, too, for attending places of amusement, for writing and producing their own plays. Literary, æsthetic, philanthropic aims all figure also, though not so often now as they will a couple of years later.

Utilization of the gang spirit.—The five chief activities of groups must be remembered when we set about enlisting children in social service. Physical activity there must be for the boys, and a surety of fun and enjoyment for both boys and girls. Roaming, hunting, and fighting can be provided for, in sublimated forms when we consider that the church fights not against flesh and blood but against the powers of darkness and wickedness. Eleven- and twelve-year-old squads make most efficient aids in running down violators of civic regulations. With their help public spirit has been aroused to improve sanitary conditions in the streets. They have canvassed for signatures to favor park beautifying or to destroy disease-bearing vegetation. They have given publicity to schemes for provision for the sick, old, and helpless in the community. In enlisting children in work of this kind we must remember to select a few natural leaders and let them pick their own groups, rather than recruit them severally and individually. As intergroup competition develops, it must be directed towards getting the best record, in quality and permanence of work as well as in the amount done.

FOR DISCUSSION

1. What results were obtained from the fore-exercise to this chapter? What growth in the ideas of patriotism is seen between nine and twelve years old?

2. How could gang loyalty be harnessed into service for civic loyalty in your community?

3. What is the disadvantage to children of Junior age of having the older boys and girls at the high school in a different building, as is so often the case?

4. It is said that women would not be so rude to each other as they are if they had been apprenticed to the fellowship of the gang in these formative years. Why might this be true?

5. In what ways do Boy Scouts and Girl Scouts utilize and develop gang loyalty? Is there a branch of these, or one for the younger "Cubs" in your neighborhood?

6. [1] "The common mistake is to pick out the proper number of boys of about the proper age, but with small regard to their other qualities and out of these to form a class. . . . It is not a natural group, and it never develops the internal structure of a real gang. There may be too many natural leaders. There may be too few. . . . More commonly, the class contains a considerable fragment of one gang, with one or two individuals out of several others, and perhaps an occasional outlier who belongs to none. The remainders of the broken gangs are in other Sunday Schools. Thus

---

[1] Quoted from Puffer's "The Boy and His Gang," where speaking of Sunday Schools, page 166.

the class remains always at cross-purposes with the boys' native impulses; and rarely, therefore, wins their instinctive loyalty.

"The remedy is . . . organize . . . on the basis of natural affiliations. Found each on some spontaneous group. Add, if you think it wise, some boys whose ganginess is less developed. But don't put fragments of well defined gangs together."

Discuss this suggestion.

7. Puffer also says:[1] "The teacher, then, in dealing with boys, must learn to think in terms of gangs as well as in terms of individuals. She must, in certain cases, go even further than this, and think of gangs entirely and not of individuals at all." Why? And can you illustrate "in certain cases"?

8. How does working together toward a common goal help develop the gang spirit?

9. What does the boy who does not belong to a gang miss in the way of character-training?

---

[1] Page 185.

CHAPTER IX

INDIVIDUALITY

FORE-EXERCISES

1. Review Chapter III for differences in mental capacity, Chaper IV for differences in physical growth, Chapter I for sex differences in play, Chapter VIII for sex differences in gang adherence.

2. Think of the two most unusual children you know. Write down the chief characteristics of each, and compare. Can you tell at all the probable cause of these differences?

3. Character-rating. It is instructive to rate a child for different qualities. Practice this in the following way. First fix in your mind a scale of five degrees. A rating of 3 is to represent an average amount of a quality; a rating of 1 would mean something that is unusually conspicuous in a child; a rating of 5 something conspicuous for its absence or the presence of its opposite. In between would come a rating of 2, meaning superior, above average but not extremely remarkable, and a rating of 4 meaning inferior, below average but not absolutely lacking. Get this fivefold scale clearly in mind.

Then select one child, consider him carefully and rate him on this scale for each of the fifteen qualities: conscientiousness, dependability, even temper, obedience, unselfishness, will power, industry, persistence, courage, control of emotions, cheerfulness, sense of humor, initiative, leadership, social adaptability. Put these in a column and allow spaces for your scale steps, mark in each rating with a heavy vertical line. Then connect these vertical lines with light horizontal lines,

and you will have what is called a character profile.
Here is a sample of one for a twelve-year-old girl:

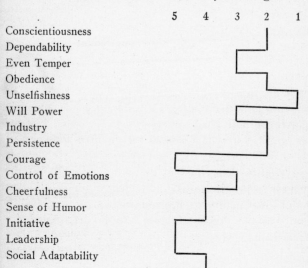

	5	4	3	2	1
Conscientiousness					
Dependability					
Even Temper					
Obedience					
Unselfishness					
Will Power					
Industry					
Persistence					
Courage					
Control of Emotions					
Cheerfulness					
Sense of Humor					
Initiative					
Leadership					
Social Adaptability					

This gives us graphically where Anna is weak or
strong—in the opinion of the one judging her. The
further to the right, the stronger Anna is; the further
to the left the weaker she is in that trait. We can see
quickly where she is strong, and where weak.

If you think wise, you might ask the day-school
teacher, and the parents, even the child himself, to
make a similar series of judgments. Explain very
clearly just what you want done, and why. Then make
the profile charts, and compare how far you all agree.

To deal comprehensively with the topic of individuality we should need to take up every phase of child
life, and point out, not the general characteristics of

the majority, but the directions in which individuals tend to differ, and the extremes they may reach. Further, we should need to consider all the multifarious combinations of character traits that might conceivably occur, and as we actually find them exhibited in various children, with, further still, degrees of difference observable due to the relative strength of these several traits. Such a task is most fascinating, but almost endless. To set some limit to our survey let us first consider the main causes of individual differences, and secondly, some special lines in which to look for the manifestations of these differences.

Heredity as a cause of individuality.—One of the biggest factors in causing individual differences is that of original nature as determined by race, nationality, and family. What children are is determined for them in large measure by the many ancestors of their race and nation. To their general make-up their parents, grandparents, great-grandparents, and progenitors further back still but in ever-decreasing potency, have contributed. Occasionally we see a "throwback," where a child seems to resemble some fairly remote ancestor in face or form, perhaps in temperament too, if tradition holds good; but more often they resemble their more immediate forbears. Of course, as you object at once, all six or eight children of one set of parents are not precisely alike, though they have the same ancestors. No more are a whole litter of pups born all at one time, still less, children, born at separate times. Here the law of variation comes in, and the law of chance selection among the infinite possible combinations of traits. But the fact remains that characteristics are handed down, the uncontrollable ones such as blue eyes, the improvable characteristics such as musical capacity, and the vaguely described traits such as ability to manage other people. No wonder, then, it pays to get acquainted with the fathers and mothers of your children, so that you may take stock, as it were, of the material you have to deal with. Some facts about the family history would also be enlightening if you could secure them; for instance, if there are eminent people in the ancestry, or peculiar people, neurotic people, very superior people in one direction, markedly inferior in another, and so forth. If there have been very opposing, and very strong, traits among the ancestors there is the greater likelihood of considerable differences among the children, or even of conflicting tendencies in one child.

That these variations are real and important may be realized in comparing the children in one family as they appeared at some given age. In spite of the similar home training they receive from conscientious and consistent parents, brothers and sisters do differ very widely, so we can judge how strong the original nature must be, with its many varieties of mixtures of traits. Here are slight pictures of five children in one family as they each were at ten years old. Jessie was shy, timid, sensitive, thought and moved slowly, could hardly ever see a joke. She was above her normal grade in school, but slow and painfully conscientious in her work. She had almost no sense of rhythm, could not sing in pitch but was most ambitious to learn the violin. She was dreamy, and forgetful of promises. Her brother Frank at ten was timid to the point of physical cowardice. He was apt to take strong dislikes to people, could be easily exasperated into fits of stubborn anger. He showed some originality of thinking, but no idea of accepting responsibility. He seldom showed any initiative, was not good in sports. He was absolutely truthful, and the soul of honor in word and deed. He played the piano moderately well and could sing very well. John at the same age showed a quiet thoughtfulness for other people, and more good judgment in practical matters than Jessie may ever attain. He had a sunny, even, good temper, and great ability to get on with other people. He had a much more pleasing voice than Frank, but far less interest in music. He was very self-willed. He was good, though not markedly superior, in school studies, but above the average in sports and physical endurance. A sister, Cora, had a school record barely up to average, and very slight musical ability. She had a strong sense of justice, albeit she was greedy and lazy. She managed other people very well, could size up a situation with good judgment. She shirked work and shirked responsibility, though she liked to domineer over her companions. Another sister, Madge, was a boisterous tomboy, afraid of nothing and nobody, impulsive and quick, full of fun and merriment. She was unusually bright at school work, but was too impatient to work for finished results. She could sing extremely well, and would have played the piano well had she ever applied herself to practice. She was quite willing to trick or cheat to get her own way, but did not often do so, as others gave in readily to her winning charm. Jessie's brooding indecision would be as foreign to her as Frank's fits of temper.

These differences persist, and become more marked as the children get older, in spite of the home training. The ideals and habits these brothers and sisters have in common may be due to heredity or to the environment of a cultured Christian home—who can tell? There is a fairly strong physical resemblance, undoubtedly due to heredity. Are the obedience, the courtesy, the good table manners, the ideas of sanitation, the happy, clean fun, the interest in each other's concerns, which characterize them all, not due to the wise fostering care of the father and mother?

Differences due to environment.—When we compare children from different homes, certain traits seem to have been developed, some habits acquired as a result of the training, or lack of it, they have experienced. Here is Elizabeth, typically "spoiled." She expects her own way all the time, has never learned to attend promptly and obey, has been encouraged to show off and attract attention, so that now she seems unpleasantly pert. Roy has no manners or social etiquette whatever; he is belligerently rude in a crowd. Powell is quiet, almost colorless at home, with perfect table manners and instant compliance with requests. Among his friends he is the ringleader in mischief, plotting many escapades of a most satisfying sort. He fits his habits to the particular environment that is responsible for training him.

Temporary adjustments to environment.—This is an important fact to remember, that training received in one line will not necessarily be transferred to another—that habits formed to suit certain people will not necessarily carry over to the adjustments to be made to other people. Thus, children trained to be polite to their teacher may be rude to their aunt; those who are overbearing at home may be submissive in the gang. It is only as the sort of habits of reaction are demanded in all sorts of varied situations that what we might call a generalized habit is formed. It is only as we foster emotional attitudes which call for these same actions no matter what the environment, that we can expect children to appreciate the ideal behind the habit; and only as we consciously widen the field of possibility where habits formed in narrow lines would be appropriate, that we can speak of certain traits as characteristic of a child. Thus, what is a courteous child? One who has several dozen specific habits of speech and action formed to guide him when with all sorts of adults, relatives, strangers, foreigners, of varied social status, age, and either sex. The emotional attitude binding all these specific acts into the abstract idea of courtesy is that of "in honor preferring one another." Now, if a child has not had this emotional tone consciously brought to his attention, and if he has received training in a few specific items only, his deportment in those special lines may be beyond criticism, while in the untutored lines he appears boorish, ill-bred, rude. This is quite likely to be the case in the Junior period, since ideals do not function very largely in children's thinking, and as yet they cannot, in the nature of things, have had the wide and varied experience that would enable them to form all the specific habits which they need. So too with other generalized habits of obedience, punctuality, unselfishness and the like. We should keep this in mind, therefore, in describing children, especially if we have seen them under a constant, prescribed set of conditions only; and try to say definitely under what circumstances we know they will act thus and so, rather than speak in vague, general terms.

Differences due to age.—A third general cause of individual differences is that of age. Even within the short span of years from nine to twelve we see changes brought about simply by growing older. Our boys and girls ready to graduate into the next department are in many respects different from the children they were when they came from the Primary. As these changes have been noted in each chapter we will simply recall a few of them here. Where nine-year-olds may be collecting marbles, the older ones are collecting birds' eggs or stamps, and find radio outfits increasingly absorbing. At nine, history is an unassorted mass of stories; at twelve it is oriented somewhat in chronological sequence. The older girls are ceasing to care about dolls, and the older boys are merging their individual selves with the corporate individuality of the gang. Fairy stories have given way to other forms of narrative, fact as well as fiction. Memory work becomes constantly easier all through this period; judgment needed in reasoning is much improved. Abstract ideas

are formed to some slight extent by twelve, thus facili-
tating general comprehension, also self-control from
ideals.

Differences due to sex.—Another cause of individual differences is the fact that some tendencies seem
much stronger than others according to whether the
subject is male or female. The mere fact of being a
boy or a girl means that some interests are likely to
prove more compelling than others. This is more true
in the Junior age period than for children who are
much younger. Since many of these differences have
been noted under each topic considered in previous
chapters, they will be merely summarized here. Boys
care more for things, and for machinery, than girls.
Girls care more for people and for decorative appear-
ances. This shows in many ways in their play and in
their reading. Boys are more active and independent,
fight more, mix better with their own kind. Girls are
more personal in their likes and dislikes, more demon-
strative and voluble in their affection, feel the group
solidarity less strongly. Their protective tenderness
frequently reaches out to babies and quite small children; they make pets of cats and birds, where boys
much prefer dogs. They mostly profess a horror, even
now, of worms, toads, snakes and the like, while boys
are interested in them, and seldom feel such repug-
nance. Before ten and a half or eleven, boys are taller
and heavier than girls; after that the reverse is true.
Boys have a greater vital index at any age; girls are
anatomically older at any age. Girls mature earlier
than boys, few beginning this process before twelve.

Ways in which individuality shows.—There are four main directions in which to look for important individual differences, one is in imagination, another is in volition, another is in disposition or temperament, the fourth is in general intelligence. A fifth, that of "goodness," may be the object of our special interest, but it is somewhat a resultant of these other things. Mere physical differences will be omitted from consideration here; the rest will be discussed in order.

Differences in imagination. — Though on the whole this is a realistic, matter-of-fact period, with well-developed ability to distinguish between the imagined and the real, yet children enjoy a good deal of vivid, visual mental imagery. Some picture to themselves the adventures described in the thrilling literature they favor, and are disappointed in any artist's interpretation; others much prefer to see real pictures, either in the book or on the screen. Some few hardly ever think in terms of visual imagery, and cannot understand those who talk confidently of mental scenery. Children with few companions frequently retain an imaginary companion from earlier years, and play a sort of serial-story daydream with invented characters. Some have little or no fancies of this type, others can spin yarns as fantastic as "Alice in Wonderland," and find themselves as much in demand among other children as was the jongleur of old at the castle gate.

Differences in volition.—Though this is chiefly an impulsive age, some children are obviously of the slow, pondering type, finding it hard to act quickly if two sides of the question are presented, and becoming almost paralyzed into inaction if several issues are to be considered. Others may be slow because of real inertia. They never seem really waked up to interested action, gripped by an idea of their own; they work up no enthusiasms, and wait always for their cue from some one else. If left to their own responsibility they wait, helplessly passive, unless some mechanical habit comes to their aid. The majority rush hastily into action, perhaps because of the real dynamic force of the impelling idea, perhaps because they cannot be bothered to take the time to think.

Some children are domineering and self-seeking to the point of being bullies. This, curiously enough, is no indication of a strong will but more likely a camouflage for very different feelings beneath. These feelings may be a profound self-distrust, a sense of inferiority, a fear of not being accepted socially, that is concealed by braggart behavior. Again it may cloak a morbid desire to be cruel, which should lead you to suspect a neurotic tendency, with probable complications in the sex life later on if not straightened out in early years.

Differences in temperament.—A third way in which individuality shows is in the general disposition. Some are evenly balanced, some very easily upset and excitable, some so extraordinarily placid that you wonder if they are ever moved to anger, grief, mirth or any other feeling. Apart from this quickness or slowness of emotions children differ in the intensity of the emotion they feel. And as the quickly moved child may be either deeply or superficially affected, and the slow, stolid child the same, that makes at least four extreme types of combination, with all sorts of gradations in between. Further, there are the brooding, self-centered, suspicious children, real trouble makers in a group, if indeed they ever manage to stay in a group at all. And there are the cocksure, happy-go-lucky, sanguine children, always convinced they and everything else will be all right, never willing to believe things have turned out wrong. They are really just as self-centered as the last lot, but seldom get the credit for it, since they are easy to get along with, and win their way by sheer fascination of other people with much the charm of a graceful cat.

Differences in intelligence.—These have been indicated in Chapter III, where we saw that our Juniors might be anywhere in school grades from the second to the tenth. Here is a boy aged ten chronologically, barely eight mentally, who has attended school for four years, but still cannot do the work of the third grade. His teachers describe him as stubborn and sullen, but he plays games well. Here is a girl aged ten, mentally nearly fourteen, doing excellent work in the seventh grade. Both adults and children find her charming and likable. We could easily pair cases more extreme than these. The vocabulary of the duller children is small and poor, that of the brighter ones is always large, sometimes amazingly so. While the slower children seldom care much for reading, and then are content with a few simple stories, the quicker ones by eleven or twelve may be found reading Shakspere, Dickens, Mark Twain, Eugene Field, Scott,

Irving, books of history, nature study, the encyclopedia, and so forth. It is interesting that in a character rating such as was suggested in Fore-Exercise 3, made on fifty mentally superior children under Terman's direction, the qualities that both parents and teachers agreed on as being conspicuously present were will power, persistence, dependability, and studiousness. It would be instructive to see how fifty mentally inferior children would be rated on these same qualities. Other evidence goes to show that the more intelligent people are also morally superior; but we cannot reverse this statement and say that the best people morally also rank high intellectually.

About one to two out of every hundred you teach will be so superior in intelligence that they stand a fair chance of rising to eminence on that score alone. But whatever their diversity, this we know surely, that the swindlers, the libertines, the criminals, as well as the Edisons, Hoovers, Sarah Bernhardts, Isabel Hampton Robbs of to-morrow are among our Juniors of to-day. How soon and how helpfully can we discover them?

FOR DISCUSSION

Think of ten children who are known to all of your discussion group. Arrange them in a rank order for each of the qualities suggested below, and as many more as you might choose. Score the one who possesses most of the quality 1, the next 2, the next 3. Score the one who possesses least of the quality, or who is most like the adjective after the word "not," 10, the next lowest 9, the next 8. Score the middle four simply M. Arrange your ranking scores as shown in the sample below. Here Amy is most courteous, Jim the least.

Billy is the most truthful, Doris the least. Nora is
the most cautious, Mary the most heedless, and so on.
Look at the characteristics of Amy and Jean for contrast, Billy and John. Would you like Mary? Frank?

	Amy	John	Nora	Frank	Bob	Mary	Jim	Doris	Billy	Jean
Courteous, not rude........	1	M	M	2	M	9	10	8	3	M
Truthful, not deceptive....	3	9	M	M	8	M	M	10	1	2
Cautious, not heedless.....	M	M	1	2	8	10	M	M	3	9
Persistent, not vacillating...	3	9	10	1	M	M	M	2	M	8
Responsible, not negligent....	3	M	8	1	M	10	M	M	2	9
Attentive, not careless.....	1	8	M	3	M	9	M	2	M	10
Independent, not suggestible	M	M	8	M	9	2	3	1	M	10
Buoyant, not morose......	2	9	8	M	M	3	10	M	M	1
Generous, not stingy......	3	M	10	9	M	1	8	M	2	M
Courageous, not timid.......	M	M	10	M	1	2	M	8	3	9
Pure-minded, not lewd....	2	10	M	M	M	8	9	M	1	3
Even tempered, not unstable.	M	M	3	2	M	9	M	M	1	10

   Compare your judgment with that of the others
in the group.

CHAPTER X

THE RELIGIOUS LIFE

FORE-EXERCISES

1. There is some evidence to show that between eleven and twelve, and for a longer period in the case of boys, children prefer the Old Testament to the New. What facts presented in Chapter V might account for that?

2. Did you ever invent a deity or a worship ritual of your own? If so, how old were you? Have you ever known children to do this?

3. Get a piece of paper, and write down the very first picture that comes to your mind as you read the following phrases. Do not pick and choose among several interpretations that may come up, but put down something descriptive of the very first idea that occurs. (Do not read over these phrases before you get that paper and are ready to write.)

(*a*) She is very religious. (*b*) That man is a saint if ever there was one. (*c*) He is always interested in religious matters. (*d*) A holy man. How far were your presentations about religious observances, organizations, behavior, creeds and doctrines?

4. Ask two or three children, as casually and informally as you can, "What is a religious man like?" and see what answers you get.

5. See the magazine, Religious Education, for February, 1922, and read carefully the Chassell *questionnaire* there given.

Without debate the proposition is here laid down that religion is a way of living. It implies the unification of all tendencies in the light of principles which prove to be true. It involves a conscious relationship with a higher power and with one's fellows. Life, or living, is revealed in terms of behavior, which is determined by the knowledge and feelings behind it. Religious life, then, must take account of ideas, emotions and actions. Religious life, however, is not to be identified with ideas about theology and knowledge of the Bible, nor with tendencies to ecstasy of devotion, nor with acts universally recognized as having to do with religion, for instance, prayer, fasting, worship ceremonial, seclusion for meditation, sacrifice. Rather, ideas must be quickened into dynamic ideals which when formulated will serve to control and direct the impulses to conduct.

We will consider first some of the emotions and ideas that contribute to religious development in general, and see which of them are natural to child life under twelve. Later we will take stock of the traits prominent in the Junior age to see which may help, and which may hinder, the most favored growth.

Feelings and emotions.—An emotion typically "religious" is that of awe and reverence, compounded, as some explain, of fear, wonder, admiration and gratitude. Do Juniors experience this sort of emotion? They do feel wonder, mostly in the form of a curiosity which drives them to investigate and explore. Fear they are learning to despise, control or conceal. Fear of social consequences bulks largely in control of behavior by the age-group standards. Awe in the sense of respect before the mysterious and unknown is found occasionally, chiefly in the presence of something over-whelmingly big or different in nature, such as the ocean, tall trees in the woods, the world revealed under the microscope, a great conflagration, the presence of death. Respect and admiration are felt for personality in a concrete hero rather than for ideas or symbols. Children have no difficulty in sharing a ritual tribute to some illustrious individual, even if it be a solemn rather than a jubilant tribute. At festivals or other special occasions their dramatic sense, or even their love of display may guarantee appropriate conduct. Frequently, however, we adults look for evidences of their being impressed, for respectful behavior, for reverence and similar traits, and find instead a careless, matter-of-fact happy-go-lucky attitude, if not a spirit of irreverence and mischief. Children are volatile, with easily distracted attention; they are very restive physically, full of spirits, greatly desirous of fun and excitement. These competing tendencies may function at the very time we should prefer a reverent expression, or at least externally decorous behavior. How-ever, children are quick to respond to the contagion of genuine awe and reverence around them, sharing in the emotion and comporting themselves in tune there-with spontaneously and easily. They also as quickly detect the spuriousness of mere outward conformity, and rebel as spontaneously by being bored, or by dis-playing irreverent deportment. Gratitude, the other component in reverence, is imperfectly developed. True, the habit of expressing thanks may be well formed, and there may be "a lively sense of favors to come," as some one has defined gratitude. They may also have been taught to think of God as the Giver, but it is seldom that these outwardly impressed forms of words have penetrated to influence the real emotional life of the ten- to twelve-year-olds. They take life, health, food, clothes, shelter for granted. Some of these, and their playthings too, come obviously from near-by sources, so that God as Giver is very far removed from actual experience, and to call him so may be considered a concession to convention.

Another feeling prominent in religious development may be described as an unrest, a consciousness of duality in our own nature, an opposition, a lack of harmony, an inadequacy of endeavor, a sense of sin, of guilt; therefore there is need of peace, of unification of this duality, resolution of the opposition, a keynote, a supporting force, a Saviour, a Redeemer. Now it cannot be said that children are troubled by these emotional problems, that they feel any pressing need for adjustment personally or socially, that they are concerned about their own unrighteousness or their souls' salvation. It is in the adolescent period, which is so much more subjective and personal, rather than in these childhood years, that we may look for this phase of development.

A third feeling contributing to religious growth is that of sympathy with suffering. We have seen that this is present, more strongly in girls than in boys, but that it is often hidden by the opposing tendencies to be cruel, to tease, to manipulate, to see others get excited. Care and responsibility for younger chil-

dren and animals, for helpless, or for old people helps
to quicken this sympathy.

A fourth distinctively religious feeling is that of fellowship. The desire to belong is strengthening all
through this period, as shown in the impulse to form
clubs and gangs. Through the experiences shared in
common, the motives, the interests felt by all, the work
done together towards a common goal, is developed the
capacity for being rooted and grounded in love, for
that social sharing which marks the citizens of God's
kingdom.

Two other instincts, those of sex and the æsthetic
interest, play no small part in the emotional side of
religion. These two are relatively weak at present compared with what they will be later on, and weak, too,
compared with other instincts that are functioning.
But since girls are more mature than boys after eleven
years old, we find some of them responsive to new
thrills and appeals before twelve. We have remarked
that those who are physiologically older are the best
prepared for religious awakenings. With even the
beginnings of the maturing processes there are corresponding changes in the emotional life. Thus, these
more advanced girls may feel a strange longing to de-
vote themselves sacrificially to a cause. There follow
romantic picturings of suffering martyrdom as a missionary, of becoming a nun, of being a princess benevolent. Fancy revels in accessories of beautiful
saintly faces, pure white robes, pious attitudes. They
may even indulge in sentimental orgies of weeping
over tales of misery, and be intrigued for a time by

books of the goody-goody order. Their inner being perceives for the first time the beautiful in architecture, in sculpture, in painting. The combination of unusually fine music, the heavy perfume of Easter flowers, the special decorations, the more elaborate ceremonial, may raise them to a seventh heaven of inward rapture comparable to Peter's state of mind on the Mount of Transfiguration. Under such conditions they are highly susceptible to suggestion, a fact much utilized by those professional evangelists who hold revival services and work with children. Some boys are likely to experience religious awakenings in this period, too. Of eighty-four selected cases studied by Coe, fifteen occurred at ten, eleven or twelve years old. But, as we shall see later, these are less often due to emotional stirrings than to a growth in self-realization.

Formation of ideas.—Let us remember that we are not born with any thoughts; all ideas that we possess have been acquired. Just what ideas a child has, then, will depend on what he has been taught. We have very few actual experiments to discover what ideas children might obtain if no definite instruction is given them. We have numberless neglected children to be sure; statistics show us that in big cities only about one child in four attens Sunday school, and we can safely conclude that a large proportion of children receive no specific religious teaching at home. In such cases children pick up stray pieces of information, oftentimes very scanty. But of course ethical standards are vaguely set up, and some crude system of philosophy shapes itself from the time the four-year-old questioner gets replies about origins and causes of things. Curiosity about birth and death may have led to speculations about immortality, divine origin and so on; but as a rule children between nine and twelve are too busily engaged with concrete objects and the pressing nature of the occupations of their social group to spend time in the contemplation of these abstract themes.

At the other extreme from the untaught children are those who have been much indoctrinated from earliest years. Their ideas necessarily reflect whatever teaching they have received. Thus, God may be to them: (1) A Creator, responsible for all that exists in nature. (2) A wonderful magic Worker producing marvels. (3) A vague Being who demands certain inexplicable conventions from us, who requires certain formulæ to be used in approaching him. (4) Some One who must be placated, sacrificed to. (5) A Spy, a Judge apt to punish severely. (6) A benevolent, rather old Person who may be persuaded into letting our desires come true. (7) An unseen Friend and Father who will guide us. His interests and aims are worth discovering and adopting; he will require work from us to help realize these aims. With any of these ideas may go a quite unquestioning faith.

Here are some "thoughts about God" obtained verbatim from fairly well instructed children. Nine and ten years: "He is very good to us." "He is very wonderful, and helps us in many ways." "He likes children to be good." "He is a very great leader." "He is kind to the sick and poor." "He sits on a throne dressed in a white robe." "He is a holy spirit who gives us love." "God is liked by people who are like him." "He likes people not to lie or steal, and to be good and obey him." Eleven and twelve years: "I see a vision in a white gown, sitting as a king on a throne surrounded by angels." "He is good and loving and likes us to be good." "He has power to heal and better the world." "He is a protector who loves us." "He wants us to do right." "He is an old man dressed in white, with long flowing hair, and wears sandals." "He is a great heavenly spirit, and a leader loving and kind." "He helps you when you're in trouble or sad." Similarly with their ideas about Jesus. Apart from creeds they may have memorized, or stereotyped phrases given given them such as our Shepherd, our Saviour, God's Son, we find that the gospel stories have taken hold of the imagination. Most Juniors have a dual conception, one of a historical character who was first a dear little Baby, then a Man who was good to people and helped them, loved children, and was shabbily treated by his friends and countrymen. The other idea is that of Some One whose name we use in prayer, sing about, perhaps pray to, who is somehow living now, rather vaguely in a place called heaven, and simultaneously, and rather unintelligibly, in our hearts.

So also with their thoughts about prayer, the Church, life after death. There are so many varieties of teaching to which they may have been exposed, and they are naturally so reticent at this age, that it is far from easy to discover what they really do think. Besides, they are not yet able to coördinate and generalize their thinking, and still less able to express themselves systematically. When pressed for a formulation we notice a tendency of the eleven- and twelve-year-olds to be wary. They preface their statements with such phrases as "I have been told that maybe it's——." "They say that——." "I have heard that——." Their desire for reality, their impatience with mere fairy-tale elements, their disillusionment in many fields makes them skeptical of some things they are told. Stories contrary to their own proved experience may be received with complete incredulity. The eleven-year-old girl, who on reading John 6:15-21 remarked, "I just don't believe that, it couldn't have happened," is typical of many who have been allowed to grow without any bias to belief one way or the other. A more reflective, somewhat older boy hesitatingly opined that "some of those stories can't be true. I guess that's just how people in those times explained things, and then they told it a lot of times and it got exaggerated." Even a ten-year-old, consistently taught that God was a loving Father, greeted the story of Elisha and the bears with, "It can't be true; God wouldn't do things like that," showing a critical faculty stimulated by the incompatibility of the ideas presented.

Development of abstract ideas.—Probably you found in working through Fore-Exercise 3 that your first spontaneous thoughts did not agree with your better judgment. Perhaps you had fleeting glimpses of someone who went to church very often, or read a great many little devotional books, or wore a seraphic, otherworldly facial expression, or was prominent in several religious organizations. Very likely these feelings and ideas originated in some childhood concept; and the chances are that your children to-day hold very similar ideas as to what constitutes religion or the religious life. What results did you get from Fore-Exercise 4?

We must remember that abstract ideas are built up from separate concrete experiences. Children associate meanings with words according to the special occasion when they heard the term used. Thus, an eleven-year-old asked to explain what "pity" meant, said, "She lost her pocketbook; it was a pity." Now if they have heard the word "religion" used only in connection with types of observances, with the recital of creeds and liturgies, with going to church, their idea of its meaning will be limited to that extent. Abstract ideas as such are but vaguely appreciated even at twelve years old; and as many of the terms in the vocabulary of hymns, prayers, and catechisms are abstract, we must realize that children have a very imperfect grasp of the generalizations they represent, a one-sided, narrow understanding of just such a concrete illustration as has been used in explanation. Consider the terms *faith, grace, justification, sin, mercy, holiness, hallowed, incarnation, salvation, atonement, redemption,* not to mention doctrines which have been the focus of controversy through the centuries. What can children under twelve make either of these or of the explanations the theologians have formulated? To be sure, they obediently memorize a prescribed form of words, but what in the way of ideas do they have behind these words? Very little, or else conceptions so amazingly grotesque that we might prefer they had been without any. From any studies made of the actual content of the minds of children below twelve we may safely conclude that whatever argument may be adduced from the churchman's wish to inoculate early, there is no argument whatever from child nature to warrant the teaching of abstract theological doctrines.

Acts of religious observance.—The list of actions given earlier contains almost nothing that seems to develop spontaneously very far in children of this age. Untaught children do not feel impelled to fast, to offer prayers and sacrifices, and so forth. They may organize some outline of ritual appropriate to their group activity, initiations or incantations similar to the counting-out rhymes; but even then we cannot be sure there is not some element of tradition, some example they have read about or observed. Children who have contact with festive occasions delight in imitating ceremonies. Playing wedding, or preacher, or funeral is a common amusement of the younger children. If they have attended Sunday school and church we may find dramatizations of baptism, confirmation, communion, but not always without a shuddering question on the part of a few as to whether or not it is impious. It is not easy to decide what is legitimately a game and how much is in earnest. Gertrude and Isabel, isolated in convalescence, decided to hold their own worship service. They arranged the room to suit them, chose hymns and Scripture selections, sermonized with avidity, but were suddenly hesitant when it came to prayer. Where was the line between the pretended and the real?

Religion as life shown in action they have of course shared from infancy's hour. But, as stated already, very few at this age realize the need for organizing life, for unifying dualities, for guiding conduct consistently by ideals.

Traits prominent.—Let us now briefly review some of the outstanding characteristics of child nature in this Junior age which are of significance for religious training. Among those which are distinctly helpful are: (1) Their admiration for heroic characters; (2) their own willingness to do and dare almost anything, coupled with a restive energy; (3) tender emotion; (4) beginnings of social groupings in which moral lessons of prime importance are being learned, as for instance, loyalty to the leader and to the group, the necessity of sharing, the value of playing fair; (5) their clearer sense of time, which is a necessary constituent in the feeling of responsibility, in tracing effects to causes; (6) the readiness with which they can be trained in deeds of service. Investigation into their ideas of right and wrong shows that they have found out, by individual suffering and by group experience, that it is wrong to be cruel, to tell tales, to cheat, to shirk one's share of labor. They increasingly feel group responsibility for mistakes and misdeeds, though they object strenuously to having the group punished for the fault of one who does not own up. They are gradually growing away from their earlier idea of punishment as mere retaliation; if called on, however, to decide on a form of punishment they often devise very neat, logical penalties for a misdemeanor, much more severe than the adult counselor of the self-government group may deem wise. They are growing toward the idea of reasoning with individuals, of finding ways that will be effective in preventing a recurrence of the act.

Among the less helpful characteristics of the period is the strong individualism, which facilitates habits of selfish heedlessness. When these habits combine with their quick impulsiveness and love of excitement, we have only too often what works out as disrespectful, mischievous, antisocial behavior. Along with planning to get their own way we find frequently a deliberate deception. This, coupled with the feeling that a lie is all right for outsiders though all wrong for friends, and with the thieving, marauding exploits of many gangs, gives the period a very doubtful reputation for honesty. Among the boys there is an indecency of language, an indulgence in low jokes, a love of making obscene sketches or scrawling upon fences and walls all sorts of filthy suggestions, frequently a practice of dirty habits all the more pernicious because it is secretive. Among the girls there is an incredible vocabulary of spite, a tendency to tell tales, to be mean, to delight in seeing another made miserably uncomfortable.

Conclusions for training.—A few suggestions as to religious training on the basis of the characteristics of the age will be in order.

We must work from their everyday life of actions and feelings rather than from ideas, symbols and abstractions. We must be practical rather than theoretical. Even before concepts are well formulated the actions and attitudes can be formed in the right direc-

tion. A few terse mottoes will often be appreciated as
slogans. Here is a double list which a Junior club
found helpful.

Stick to it until finished	No dawdling
Play fair	No shirking
Work cheerfully	No telltales
Share your good times	No dirty stories listened
Give up pleasantly	to or repeated
Be respectful	No unkind criticism
Let others' property alone	No whining
Find a way to help	No teasing others until
Find a way to give pleasure	they are unhappy.

They may be led to think about Jesus as a boy, with
his life of work, learning and games, and to imagine
how he probably acted in situations similar to those
which they meet in their own lives.

They must have opportunities to make choices and
exercise judgment. Some simple form of self-government in the club group is indicated for all but the
youngest in the department.

Clean, reverent sex knowledge must be given early
enough to set up a healthy attitude and forestall the
soiling of the mind from impure sources.

Their sympathies and imagination must be aroused
by illustrations of worth-while, heroic characters, while
ways of imitating are tactfully pointed out.

Chances for deeds of service must be afforded, and
contact with widening groups assured until they feel
kinship with all sorts and conditions of people.

Working out from the sense of loyalty, and the desire to belong, we may present, to the eleven- and twelve-year-olds more particularly, the suggestion of expressing loyalty to Jesus the supreme Hero, and of belonging to the organized group of disciples and friends in the church.

FOR DISCUSSION

1. Illustrate the force of suggestion in moral training.

2. What was wrong with the training which led children to look upon Sunday as a day when you could not do anything you liked?

3. What moral problems do children of Junior age face?

4. What definite thing has your Junior Department done during the year to train children in Christian living?

5. Using the Chassell *questionnaire,* from Religious Education for February, 1922, agree as a group upon a certain set of answers you would regard as right. After having made a survey of your department by using the *questionnaire* as suggested, tabulate and score the children's answers as agreed. What sort of religious conceptions do you find?

6. What is the value to you of such an exercise as the above?

7. Can you find out anything about the conditions under which your children pray spontaneously? What training, as well as instruction in prayer do they receive? Which children pray daily? Do they use set forms? If not, what do they pray about?

8. What have you heard your children say that would show any connection in their minds between their ideas of right and wrong and their ideas of God?

9. Give instances of children's judgments about conduct, in themselves or in others.

10. Illustrate the sort of thing that stimulates them to generosity.

11. When have you noticed instances of real self-sacrifice? Of special selfishness? Notice carefully what stimulates either, and the social setting.

12. Criticize the following statements:

(a) Knowledge which has no issue in conduct is barren, so far as religion is concerned.

(b) Children appreciate conduct only in concrete personality.

(c) Good manners form one of the best introductions to good citizenship.

(d) Moral knowledge is most meaningful when it is gained as an answer to actual problems in life.

(e) Even if children have a religious impulse they will not grow up "religious" without religious education.

A GOOD BIBLIOGRAPHY

REFERENCES PARTICULARLY FOR THIS AGE PERIOD

Cabot, Ella Lyman, Seven Ages of Childhood. Chs. VIII-XIII.

Coe, Geo. A., Education in Religion and Morals. Chs. XII-XIV.

Coe, Geo. A., Social Theory of Religious Education. Part III.

Hartshorne, Hugh, Childhood and Character. Chs. IV, VII, XI-XIII.

Kirkpatrick, E. A., The Individual in the Making. Ch. VII.

Lee, Joseph, Play in Education. Chs. XXV-XLII.

Norsworthy and Whitley, Psychology of Childhood. Chs. III, IV, VIII, XIII, XV.

GENERAL DESCRIPTION OR SUGGESTIONS FOR TRAINING

Abbott, E. H., On the Training of Parents.

Chenery, Susan, As the Twig Is Bent.

Du Bois, Patterson, Fireside Child Study.

Fisher, Dorothy C., Self Reliance.

Fisher, Dorothy C., Mothers and Children.

Forbush, William B., The Coming Generation.

Forbush, William B., The Boy Problem.

Forbush, William B., The Boy Problem in the Church.

Gruenberg, Sidonie, Sons and Daughters.

Howard, W. L., Start Your Child Right.

Kirby, J. A., That Boy of Yours.

Kirkpatrick, E. A., Fundamentals of Child Study.

Kirkpatrick, E. A., The Use of Money.

McKeever, William A., Training the Boy.

McKeever, William A., Training the Girl.

Puffer, J. Adams, The Boy and His Gang.

Tanner, Amy E., The Child.

Terman, Lewis M., The Hygiene of the School Child.

Wile, Ira S., Sex Education.

Wood-Allen, Mary, Making the Best of Our Children.

FICTION THAT WILL PROVE HELPFUL

Joseph Anthony, The Gang.

Walter Dyer, The Dogs of Boytown.

William D. Howells, A Boy's Town.

Lucy Montgomery, Anne of Green Gables.

Booth Tarkington, Penrod.

Charles D. Warner, Being a Boy.

Kate D. Wiggin, Rebecca of Sunnybrook Farm.